I'M PREGNANT,
NOT TERMINALLY ILL,
YOU IDIOT!

The cover image was shot for *Mother & Baby*, India's most loved pregnancy and parenting magazine, as part of a pregnancy fashion feature.
Photographer: Parikshit Suri
Hair & Make-up: Recinda Martis

*A baby is God's opinion
that the world should go on.*
                    CARL SANDBURG

Dedicated to
Amma (the one who birthed me)

And Re (the one I birthed)

Contents

Prologue — ix

Doing the Math	1
Fertility Politics	13
Have Bump. Will Flaunt.	29
That's My Bump. Talk to ME!	39
Thinking Good Thoughts – My Foot!	51
Sneezy, Sleepy, Woozy, Weepy, Grumpy, Happy and Farty	65
The Pregnancy Fellowship Programme	77
The Birth Mutiny	89
All About My Mother	105
Much Ado About the Boob	115
Up and About	135
S-E-X: Where it all Started	151
Maid in Heaven	161
Sisterhood of the Wailing Mommies	177
What Does Baby Do Now?	191
Myth of the Hands-on Daddy	203

Work Bitches	217
When Does It Get Better?	231
Epilogue: No one told me this	243
Acknowledgements	249

Prologue

'You will know when you become a mother,' my mother always told me.

'Why should I wait so long? Tell me now, I will understand,' the cheeky me would always retort.

'No, you won't,' she would say, almost resignedly. 'You just wait and watch.'

And so I waited.

It is very difficult to point out exactly *when* motherhood begins.

Is it when you finally decide you don't care if the bra is ugly or not, but it bloody well be comfortable?

Is it when your husband's boxers suddenly become the most comfortable underwear ever?

Is it when you suppress the urge to scream 'ASSHOLE!' at the biker who overtook you from the left in peak traffic, thinking, *What if the baby hears?*

Is it when pulling your boob out in public becomes the most natural thing to do, and you don't care if the taxi driver is taking a good look in the rear-view mirror while your partner is desperately looking for something to cover you with?

Is it when you realise that your breast is the solution to all cries, big and small?

Or does motherhood begin when, a week after you missed your period, you finally decided to take the pregnancy test?

Or when you surreptitiously bought the pregnancy kit from the chemist, rushed home to douse it with your urine, waited with bated breath for the verdict, and decided, yes, there must be something growing inside me?

Or when you were pacing up and down the house, waiting for your husband to come home so you could tell him, 'I have some news!'?

Or when you held a report in your hands that enlisted the potency of the pregnancy hormone in your body?

Or when the sonologist pointed to something on the screen and said, 'Can you see that? That is the baby's spine!'? When you squinted your eyes, trying to look intelligently at a visual you could make no head or tail of? When you mumbled a 'Yes!' just so you don't end up looking like a cold, non-maternal bitch?

Or does it all begin when you felt the first sign of movement within you? The first kick?

Or the day you ate an ice-cream cone and heard someone devouring it inside you within seconds?

Or when you suppressed the urge to run across the street with your very pregnant belly and decided to wait for the green signal instead?

Or when you were handed, along with a baby, a card that read, 'Infant of (your name here)' at the hospital, post-delivery?

Or when you turned over in bed, and decided you have to be careful, as you might roll a tiny someone else over, or crush him or her?

Or when someone infinitesimally small latched on to you and began to suckle, and you and your husband gave each other a *we-made-this* look?

It is hard to decide exactly **when** you become a mother.

But this book is not about motherhood really. For starters, it is about *you*, and not about the baby. The *you* that sometimes gets lost in the whole pregnancy and motherhood journey. The *you* that can be angry, sad, silly, excited, confused, wicked, rude, girl, slut and everything un-mommy. The *you* that is spending lonely nights, tossing around in bed with a heavy belly, while the husband is watching television. The *you* that is silently cursing, muttering, wondering why sleep is so elusive when the world is expecting you to 'talk to the baby' or 'think good thoughts'.

The *you* that sometimes looks at your significant other and wonders: Is **that** the father of my child?

The *you* that shudders to think how much your life is going to change with motherhood. And how irreversibly.

The *you* that hasn't really fathomed how to *do* motherhood.

The *you* that sometimes wants to make it all go away – the man, the marriage, the pregnancy – and be footloose and fancy-free again.

The *you* that knows that soon, your goals and ambitions may not be a priority and that you will always have to put someone else's interest before yours.

The *you* that is excited and petrified about motherhood, yet has no clue what it really means.

The *you* that will wonder (mostly in anger), *Now why didn't anyone tell me that?*

The *you* that will never be the same you again.

This book is about the Jekyll and Hyde of being pregnant. And being a mother. It's about the happy stuff, but it's also about the ugly stuff – the stuff that makes you mean, even vicious, while still feeling oodles of love for the thing you just created. The stuff that makes it okay to kill anyone who comes in your way of doing things the way you think is right for your baby.

Because it's far from rosy out there. And it's not about knowing when your 'foetus' will be the shape of a lemon, an avocado, an aubergine or a pumpkin. Or when will it grow a heart, a brain, lungs or kidneys. This book is not about finding out how to get your body or your sex life back.

I only summoned the courage to write it when my husband read a sort of chapter and told me it had him riveted. And he wasn't even pregnant.

Perhaps it should have been written during my pregnancy. Or during my baby's initial months, in *real time*, when one could feel it all, much more intensely.

Perhaps. But it would have been too raw, too real, too debilitating.

A friend even suggested I get pregnant again and do it like a diary – he just escaped getting disfigured by me.

So it took time. It took healing. It took really long to feel 'me' again.

PS: For the purpose of convenience, I have referred to the baby as 'he' in the entire book. It doesn't mean anything, except that since I gave birth to one, it is more familiar turf.

1
Doing the Math

There was a time when you met people who fell in love, got married (or at least one of the two happened), got pregnant and had babies. And then there was a time when people fell in love, but found it difficult to stay in love, got married, but found it difficult to stay married. It was the era of ambivalence, which made making babies a tad more complicated.

According to me, there are basically three kinds of scenarios in the urban babydom thing, at least among the upwardly mobile city slickers (for I belong to that group). The first is couples who marry at the 'right age' (read late twenties) when they are in the growth path of their career (and their hormones). Such couples have the luxury of intellectualising their procreation and their investments. So while enjoying 'coupledom time' (read manicured four-day vacations in Hong Kong/Bali/Maldives) they are scheduling a time when they 'will be ready'. This plan sometimes backfires. Often, the procreational gods let them down when they are most wanted, and they are left high and dry and progeny-less.

Such couples could go through ten odd years of married life, SIPs, EMIs, and suddenly stop to wonder, *Where are the babies?* This is the point when they furiously start reading 'How to get pregnant' books. The alarm bells start ringing, spurring a series of strategies, consultations, medical or spiritual interventions, even fertility treatments before they officially conceive, or sometimes, adopt.

In the second scenario (a bit of a rarity now) are couples who marry in their early twenties and make the babies quickly. This is the age when people have the most physical energy for parenting (and you do need a lot of that). But more often than not, it causes the woman to abort her just-taken-off career or life or freedom from parents midway and become the baby-caring machine for the rest of the decade, at the very least.

The flipside to this is: the kids are in college by the time you hit your forties and then you can do the 'me' or 'us' time for as long as you want – go backpacking, reinvent yourself, take a cruise, get that doctorate, whatever. I have several such friends whose kids are teenagers, and sure, it feels odd with me still chasing a toddler.

My friend Ritu got married at twenty-two and had her first baby at twenty-three. Her daughter is now eighteen, and a friend.

'When I got married, most of my friends were still dating, changing boyfriends, figuring out who they were and what they wanted to do. They just didn't get me,' she lamented, while talking about her young motherhood.

'Post-marriage, in my effort to be different Ritus to different people – my husband, my baby, my in-laws – I forgot who the real me was. It took me time to claw my way back. Once the kids grew up, my rebellion set in; I was driven by the need to prove myself. I guess there is less frustration in figuring who you are at forty.'

Ritu now wears many hats. She is an academic, has started a film club, is the director of a literary festival in her city, does a fair bit of theatre, writes poetry, and has enrolled for her PhD.

A colleague of mine, Amrita, had her first baby when I was still flitting from one wrong guy to another. She ended up being a stay-at-home mum for fourteen years before resuming her career. Her older one is fifteen now, though Amrita and I are the same age. Having wrestled with the dilemma of giving up a career to be with the kids, she did what she had to do as a mother. 'I gave it all I had. But I am back to polishing up on that resume and getting that American degree I wanted a decade-and-a-half ago. Looking back and then looking at my babies, I think I did good,' she says.

The third scenario (increasingly common among the educated, upwardly mobile metropolitan) is that of couples marrying in their late thirties. Now while they are in a good place as far as their career and finances go, they don't have the luxury of 'planning' a baby. In some cases, lifestyles have also taken a toll on their fertility (alcohol, smoking, bad diets, cholesterol, triglycerides and other demons have wreaked havoc by then). Women on prolonged birth control pills also confuse their hormones to an extent that pregnancy takes longer than usual. Such couples usually come to terms with the fact that baby-making might be complicated, or 'high-risk'. They might have even missed the baby bus or might have to adopt, do the IVF thing, IUI, human growth hormone, or whatever they can afford or are asked to do. Plus there is this thing of fitness levels and how underestimated they are.

My friend Sunaina had her kids late, between her mid to late thirties. Although she felt she was in a good place mentally when she had them, and was okay with letting work take a back seat, she also realised she didn't have the energy she had a decade ago.

'Kids involve a lot of running around, and I felt I was not equipped for it. It took a lot out of me, and I wondered how it could have been, had I had them earlier. Now they are seven and eleven and full of beans, but there's still a long way to go. My friends, on the other hand, seem at ease, since their kids are nearly twenty, and are pretty much on their own.'

If you ask me, I don't really think there's a right time to have a baby, whatever anyone else might say about the 'clock'. Unless you are a supermodel on a work contract that penalises you for getting pregnant, the right time to have a baby is when the baby wants to have you.

I was pretty sure by the time I hit my late thirties that since a good man worth making a baby with was nowhere in sight, having a baby was perhaps ruled out entirely, since the ovarian clock was going tick-tock. In a classic twist to my tale, I actually met a man I fell in love with at the age of thirty-eight. We got married within a year of dating. Luckily for me, he was a bankable sperm. I got pregnant at the not-so-naughty forty. Evidently, I had hit the jackpot.

Shock and disbelief followed. The mother got on top of things. She had pretty much given up on me, leave alone my reproductive capabilities. Maybe she assumed my ovaries would have shrunk by now. She had perhaps resigned herself to the fact that she would never be able to knit sweaters for her grandchildren. It was something she did for every newborn in the family, however random the connection. She even went as far as knitting sweaters for my friends' babies. She hoped that I would take the hint and notice the aching in her heart and have one of my own (read get married and head in that direction). It just took really long for her dream to come true.

When I announced to her that I was pregnant, she exclaimed, 'Thank Lord Ganesha! It is a miracle!' I wondered what Ganesha had to do with it and how little she credited me. But then, that's my mother.

It's simpler in the movies. All it took for a Bollywood heroine of yore to get pregnant was a stormy, rainy night, a fireplace, a man and a song. I always wondered: How is it that sexual intercourse (even if it was the first time) always happened in her ovulation window, her most fertile time of the month? How is it that the hero never suffered from lazy sperm syndrome? Or she, a lazy egg?

So what does it take to get pregnant? One might think it is the easiest thing on earth, considering that at least three million sperms enter your body during unprotected intercourse. Surely one of them should be fit enough to make a baby? But there are technicalities:

Is it the right day of the month?
Is it the right time of the day?

Are these sperms motile enough, or do they need some 'speed' to be able to make it?

Is there any sperm at all?

How lazy is your egg/ovary?

Okay, once the sperm and the egg have done their bit, do they have enough room/conditions to survive in your uterus? Is your uterus classic, deluxe, super-deluxe or a suite?

Are your numbers good? Haemoglobin, platelets, WBCs, amniotic fluid, sugar levels, thyroid, other hormone levels?

If you beat all the odds and still get pregnant, congratulations!

Back in the real world, one constantly hears about women unable to conceive. Why does that happen?

Okay, consider the odds of getting pregnant. Your fertile window is two days in a month. Okay, I know they say four days, but take it from me, it's two. In those two days, you have to have a potent man around (read a man who doesn't suffer from low sperm motility or pathetic sperm count, sheer laziness or just, non-existence).

Then, you and the said man have to have sex. Which means there has to be opportunity, availability, initiative, interest and enterprise. Then your egg has to have an affinity for his sperm and allow it to stay. Only then will you have any chance of missing that old and faithful period.

Dipali, a friend of mine who is in a high-pressure job that requires her to travel a lot, is still struggling with being in the same city as her husband while she is ovulating. After being bombarded with 'good news' queries, she finally barked, 'Yes, if we happen to be in the same city often enough, we will make the babies!'

I was talking to my friend Neil, who had recently ended his twelve-year-no-kids marriage. He was in his late forties and the pressure to be a father was looming large. 'I don't know how to start the whole relationship thing all over again. I really want kids, but I'd rather be with someone who already has them. It seems like too much work dating a single woman, getting married and fathering one on my own,' he said.

Sure, divorce feels like the clock just moved back on the parenting thing. Because now, you not only have to find a mate, but find one with whom you can make the babies quickly, as you have already lost time in your first marriage. Last heard, Neil was in a steady relationship with a woman who had a daughter from her first marriage.

A college friend, Joanne, who suffered from rheumatoid arthritis, had to take painkillers to be able to wake up every morning. After being married for eight years and being torn about having a baby, she decided to engineer her pregnancy when she hit thirty-five. So she got an okay from her doctor, got off her lifesaving painkiller drug (proclaimed life-threatening to the foetus) and started keeping an ovulation diary. There was only a small problem. She had to bully her husband to have sex with her on her ovulation days.

At the end of two years, when the pain in her knees was excruciating, but her ovary still bare, it was time for a reality check. Tests revealed that her husband had almost zero sperm motility and would need a minor surgery to fix it. Meanwhile, relatives started pouring out their condolences. So what if she couldn't conceive, she could still adopt, they said. It was time for her to shriek, 'It's not me, it's him!'

Baby Byte:
If You Made Me, You are a Statistical Wonder!

I always wonder about people who've been married long enough (read longer than five years) and haven't made the babies. That is, if they aren't part of the DINK (Double Income No Kids) brigade, which is cool by me, as long as people are honest about it and don't give the usual excuses about 'not being ready', or wanting to focus on their career or being more financially stable. My childhood friend Nisha maintained through her fourteen-year DINK state that she wasn't ready, and they weren't sure if they wanted kids. Finally, in year fifteen, they adopted a baby. I think infertility is still a touchy topic, despite IVF, surrogate moms and all that jazz.

But elsewhere in the nation, people are busy breeding every minute, and that is what makes us the country with the second-largest population in the world.

The Curious Case of the LMP

Before I conceived, I sort of figured that it would be important to record the night of the baby-making sex, just in case the information is required. Since I am the queen of trivia, I thought this would be an interesting one to document. Unfortunately, throughout pregnancy, there is absolutely no reference to this momentous day. It will always be a little secret between you and your partner. No one will ask you about it, it will not be used for any calculation and it will not be recorded anywhere for posterity.

Anyway, the-sucker-for-dates, super-organised me, was almost diligent about keeping a sex diary. This meant that every time we had unprotected sex on a day when I was allegedly 'on heat', or in my 'ovulation window', I wrote it down. The euphemism for safe days in our calendar was 'Happy Hours' and that for fertile days was 'High Voltage'.

Once, the husband and I took off for a weekend wine festival to the Sula vineyards in Nasik. I don't know if it was being away from work, or the city, or if it was the wine, the weather or the vineyard's beauty, but we were having marathon sex, two days in a row. When we came back to Bombay, I realised it had happened in the 'High Voltage' zone of my calendar. 'Oops! We could be pregnant,' I told the husband. He laughed it off.

'If we have a girl, let's call her Sula,' he said.

'What about Satori?' I humoured him. I couldn't believe he was so blasé about it.

'Too slutty.'

We debated on Dindori too (never paying heed to the fact that it could well be a boy), but finally agreed on Sula. Anyway, Sula never happened, but the third time we were in 'High Voltage', I got pregnant!

I later figured that the only number that matters in the ob-gyn world when you are pregnant is not the date of the actual baby-making sex, but your last menstrual period (LMP), which is the most boring detail one can record. I mean how many women remember the date of their LMP? No wonder most due dates are way off the mark.

Anyway, LMP will be the three most ominous letters through your pregnancy. It is what will be stated in all records and filled in forms. It is something you will be repeating over and over again each time you go for a consultation, test, sonography, hospital registration, whatever.

Baby Byte:
Someone please do something about recording my inception in more respectable terms. This LMP sounds like some locomotive project.

I'm Pregnant, Not Terminally Ill, You Idiot!

Here's the foxing bit. Usually, when you take the pregnancy test, the doctor says you are six to seven weeks pregnant. You are quite sure you didn't make-the-baby so long ago. This makes you feel as though you were pregnant even before you had the pregnancy sex (time between your LMP and the day of the romp is also taken into account). That takes two months off the nine-month pregnancy straightaway! It's as though you have earned a pregnancy discount.

I tried arguing the LMP calculation for the due date with my doctor. He would have none of it. All he said is that it was a more efficient calculating method. He believed (as did others) that women are still more likely to remember their period than their sex days. Whatever! But it somewhat challenges the whole Bollywood cliché of 'I bred you in my womb for nine months' in the classic face-off between estranged mother and son. The son is more likely to say: 'What nonsense! Tell me what your LMP was and we'll take it from there.'

2
Fertility Politics

Pregnancy is not always cute. Not to everyone. Because the one thing a pregnant woman reminds you of, in an in-your-face sort of way, is that she is pregnant and you are not. Or that she is married (for the purpose of convenience, I haven't included pregnancies out of wedlock) and you are not. Or she is fertile and you are not. Or she is having sex and you are not. Or she's in for the long haul and you are not. Or she is simply ready and you are not.

Unlike marriage, boyfriends, affairs or relationships, which can be camouflaged and on which information can be shared only on a need-to-know basis, pregnancy is out there and very public. On one hand, it makes things look bright and beautiful (at least to the couple involved). But it also changes the dynamics of relationships – at work, among friends, in your social circle, in the family – sometimes resulting in turbulence.

Women who Work Together, Bleed Together

If you have a full-time job, you'll be spending at least a third of your day at work. A pregnant woman with her belly prop somewhat rocks the oestrogen atmosphere in the space around her. When I got pregnant, it was almost like I had betrayed the rest of my ilk at work and would no longer be synchronised with their biological cycles.

It was official. I didn't belong. I was an outcast. I ate too much, peed too much, tired too easily, sat too much, felt sleepy a lot, yawned too much, and smiled a lot. No one told me any gossip anymore, hardly anyone bitched to me, no one asked me if I wanted to 'hang out' after work. People tend to think you are too zoned out to want any of this when you are pregnant.

Most other mommies at work pretended they didn't remember what it was to be pregnant (if they had a baby three or more years ago). They looked at me like I was part of some lofty science experiment. It's like smug-marrieds totally forgetting what it was like to be single.

On the other hand, to single women, I was a reality check. Is this what it will come to? Can they see themselves doing this? Or does it totally scare the shit out of them?

Pregnancy is also the time, when people you don't know at work, act like your best friends. The cleaning lady in the loo asked me, 'Good morning, madam. How are you feeling?' The girl from accounts would accost me every day, 'How many months? When are you going on leave?' And although it's a cliché, a pregnant woman always feels good on being asked the obvious. Not asking would be rude, as though you haven't acknowledged the pregnancy. Asking too much would be intrusive.

Perhaps what pregnant women hate as much as too little fuss is too much fuss. *Are you okay? Need something? A sandwich? Should I get a cushion? Is it too hot for you? Too cold for you? Can you walk the stairs? Should we get you another chair? Can you have coffee? Pizza? Blah blah blah...*

You feel like saying: 'I am pregnant, not terminally ill, you idiot!' but that wouldn't look good on you. So you clench your teeth, seethe within, and smile serenely – the smile that pregnant women tend to perfect after a few months.

People who hated you at work will hate you even more now. It's all in-your-face. The aura, the allure! The fact that they owe it to you to be nice. The fact that you can't be ignored for a long time, because it would be considered bitchy to do so.

During my early months, I wasn't really showing, nor did I have a real morning sickness. What I had instead, was an increased intolerance-for-nincompoops sickness. One morning, our marketing team was at the receiving end. They came beaming about their latest ad campaign for our paper. I told them exactly what I felt about it. It was bollocks. Not. Very. Nice. Later, the boss covered up for me by telling them I had 'hormonal problems' and was being treated for it. I had sworn him to secrecy about 'my condition'.

Baby Byte:
There is a reason it is called a foetus. It is not a virus.

A few months later, when I was visibly showing, I remember a girl from the news desk who came to my cubicle one afternoon, just as I had propped myself up with my four-course meal. She had been ignoring me all along the past few years, even though I always smiled at her.

I thought she wanted to break the ice. Instead she got to the point.
'Do you have Vishal Bharadwaj's number?'
'Not right now. But I can get it for you. Is it urgent?'
'Umm... can you email it to me by this evening? I am on Lotus. Thanks.'
She stared at me. Stared at my bump. Stared at my lunch. Nothing.

Closer to the end of my pregnancy, when I wasn't sure I was moving forwards or backwards (my centre of gravity was non-existent), she piped up again.
'Do you know any interesting people we can interview for the anniversary issue?'

'Ummm... let me think and get back to you. Can't tell off-hand. But I won't be there to see it through though.'

'Why? Where are you going?'

Nothing again. I was nine months pregnant and looked like I was going into labour any day. But nothing yet from her. Not one question.

'Umm... maternity leave (pointing to my belly).'

'Ohh... ok...'

I later found out she and her husband were desperately trying to have a baby for six years.

Then there was a chronic singleton I always met at the landing, while she was smoking. Now, while the men would act flustered and guilty whenever this happened and hurriedly put their cigarettes away, she always continued smoking. She, too, never asked me even once about my pregnancy, although I caught her cooing at baby pictures on her computer a few times.

So there are all kinds of encounters and various dialogues waiting to happen:

Pregnant woman with another married-but-not-wanting-to-be-pregnant woman.

'Don't tell me!'

'Yes.'

'How does it feel?'

'Weird, but okay.'

'Is it bad? The morning sickness thing?'

'I haven't had it, so I don't know.'

'So will you continue working?'

Pregnant woman with another married-and-wanting-to-be-pregnant-but-not-being-able-to woman.

'That was fast!'
   'I think his sperm was on speed.'
   'Good for you!'

Pregnant woman with single-but-in-a-relationship woman.

'Awww... you look so cute. Do you know if it's a boy or a girl?'
   'No, they aren't allowed to tell you.'
   'I love all those maternity dresses you wear. You must get yourself a pair of overalls. I think pregnant women look really cute in overalls...'
   'Hmm... yes, they do.'

Pregnant woman with a single-but-in-a-dead-end-relationship woman.

'Wow. At least you made a baby. I don't know a single marriage that is working.'

Pregnant woman with a single-and-no-man-in-sight woman.

'You are pregnant?'
   'Yes.'
   'I wanted to ask you, but I thought it would be rude.'
   'That's okay, now you know.'
   'So does it change things?'

Pregnant woman with man-hater.

A cold stare.

I'm Pregnant, Not Terminally Ill, You Idiot!

Pregnant woman with been-there-done-that mother of two

'Enjoy all you can now. Your life is over when the baby comes.'

Pregnant woman with eternal partyholic-singleton.

'Oh, god! So now you won't come out drinking with us?'
  'Of course I will.'
  'Wow, you are a rockstar!'

Somehow the male colleagues of a pregnant woman always look a tad embarrassed and don't know what to say or do. Like they were responsible for it or something! They are either fumbling around, or avoiding your gaze. Of course the daddies at work sort of nod in agreement and have that look of 'we know how that feels'.

The rest of the menfolk feel a sense of awe and protectiveness about you. It's a big deal to them that you are carrying a human life inside. Men who have, untill then, shown no chivalry whatsoever, will begin to do so. Chairs will be vacated, doors will be held open, and elevator buttons will be pressed till fingers hurt. Although the mind of a man is a weird place, and thought is often removed from action.

Man (thinking): She has tits.
Man (saying): Wow, congratulations! I just heard.
Or
Man (thinking): There goes my ability to flirt with her.
Man (saying): Let me get that door for you.
Or
Man (thinking): Stop thinking such thoughts. She is carrying someone else's baby.
Man (saying): So how's it going?

The Relationship Barometer

Pregnancy also implies in a rather tangential or roundabout manner that at some level you have decided, this is *it*. This is the relationship to keep. This is the guy to grow old with. This is the father of my child. At least in your head, you seem to have some clarity about how invested you wish to stay in the relationship.

Around the time I was pregnant, at least three married couples I knew went through separations after averaging six to ten years of marriage. I was shocked. These were not the obviously volatile marriages. The said couples looked socially, emotionally, intellectually and aesthetically matched. Clearly, none of them had an affair or another romantic interest as the cause of the breakup. None of them had kids either.

Any relationship where the couple is holding off on having a baby for other than financial reasons is usually under the radar, almost as much as couples who have been together for several years and not been married. I know, I am old-fashioned, but eight out of ten marriages where there is no baby in sight for over six years (provided the babylessness is a joint decision) end in separation. Unless, of course, there are a dozen dogs or cats in the foreground. Or you are a bestselling author, busy striking multi-million-dollar book deals.

My pregnancy made several smug-marrieds sit up and take stock. *Married is one thing, but pregnant? That's serious, dude.* Which made me realise: yes, having a baby is a big deal. It's a 'let's-affix-a-permanent-stamp-on-our-marriage' kind of thing.

Perhaps it's because of an oestrogen high, and all those feel-good hormones, but pregnancy makes you feel good. Sort of euphoric, once you are past the initial queasiness. From then, at least till month seven, there is a bounce in your step, a glint in your eyes, a smile on your face, a life in your belly. If marriage made you smug, motherhood makes you cocky. No matter how long someone else has been married, you made the baby! You are ahead of the game. It's true. Hierarchies among women are simple and ruthless. Single woman. Woman in relationship. Married woman. Woman with child.

Baby Byte:
Yes, I do make her look good. Look how she's flaunting me!

The Friendship Roller Coaster

When you announce you are pregnant to your friends, different things happen. Some are genuinely happy for you and show it. Some are wary, as fingers could now be pointed at them. They could be victims of the 'you-are-next' syndrome. Some are sympathetic in an 'O-my-god-your-life-is-over' kind of way. Some are peeved that they have been left behind in the womb race. Some are just anxious and full of questions about the status of the friendship. Will you now prioritise the baby over everything, they wonder. 'Are you ready for this?' they ask.

They can't get it. Last time you met, you were a serial singleton with man problems. Now you are a legitimate married and pregnant woman, about to give birth to another human being. It skews the dynamic a bit. It's not that you engineered it this way, but now the singletons seem pressured to catch up. If they had their way, they would fast-forward their life, find a man, marry him and make the babies soon.

The mommy clan among friends on the other hand welcomes you into their fray. One more to vent about parenting and other issues with, they think. The serial singletons think you are less cool. The married couples sit up and take stock of where they are headed.

The thing is, through my singledom, I was at the receiving end of many a bump – that of friends, colleagues and family – and knew exactly how that felt. I was the last one in my lot to tie the knot, so by the time I had my baby, all my peers had teenage kids at the very least, or had legitimised their DINK status.

Post-baby, a school friend of mine, who I lost touch with for over ten years, surfaced on Facebook. *Hey I see a baby in your photos. Is it yours? Did you adopt or give birth or what?* Through my single days, she was always playing the smug-married card and trying to set me up. I guess I was now the hare and she, the tortoise.

For couples ambivalent about the baby thing, a pregnant woman is a reminder that they have unfinished business. My friend Manya wore many hats – model, actress, dancer, TV show host. She was married long before me, but I figured the babies had to wait as she probably wasn't ready, with her career on such a roll. It turned out that was not the case.

'Wow, I never thought you'd have a baby so soon. How long have you guys been married?'

'A little over a year. How about you?'

'Seven years now.'

'Don't want kids?'

'I do, but Rohit doesn't. Will you ask Dee to speak to him?'

'Hmmm... are you sure? It's so personal. What can Dee say?'

'Just how good it feels to be a father. How it's all cool. Stuff like that. Men like to hear it from other men.'

Dee never had that conversation. Within a year, they had separated.

Sometimes you also inspire couples on the verge to go for it. Like we did with Sam and Neena. I did feel overwhelmed when

Neena came to visit us at the hospital twice, and made it a point to visit us at home every few months with Sam. Something was going on. When I prodded, she told me that earlier, he was ready while she wasn't, and now it was the opposite. She too wanted Dee to do the father talk with Sam. Since I figured they were almost there, I didn't push Dee.

I was right. In a few months, she called me. I already knew what was coming.

'Are you busy? Do you have time to talk?'
'It's cool, I just have a baby on my boob.'
'I have to tell you something.'
'You are pregnant!'
'And you are the first one to know.'
'YAY!'
'And you and Dee have been the chief inspiration for it!'
'So happy we were useful....'

It's All in the Family

Crass as it might sound, getting pregnant moves you up the ladder in the whole family hierarchy thing. Yes, that sounds vulgar, but procreation does increase your net worth in the family.

I had been single for so long that my relationship with my parents got worse every year and at some point, it felt irreparable. If getting married reversed the tension by fifty percent, having a baby did a complete flip and made everything seem alright. It was as though the last fifteen years had never happened.

Suddenly the mother who had given up on me was full of concern and questions.

'Hope you are eating properly? You have to eat for two, you know.'

'What nonsense, Amma. Yes, I am eating well.'

'Also, you must be calm now. Don't lose your cool. Don't carry work stress home. It's not good for the baby.'

'Hmmm... okay, whatever.'

'Want me to make something and bring? Sheera? Coconut barfi? Gajar ka halwa? Any pickle?'

'No, Amma, I'll tell you if I need anything. Right now I have no such cravings.'

The father who hardly ever called was now calling me. Me?

'So how are you?'

'What happened to me? I am fine.'

'All reports, everything okay?'

'Ya, Appa. All good.'

'Right, then. Look after yourself!'

An uncle who I hadn't spoken to in ages sent me an e-greeting, congratulating me. Another one wanted to add me as a friend on Facebook. Cousins who had been procreationally active got in touch and offered their two bits. I was in demand! My family loved me!

It's like the whole ecosystem around you changes. All in anticipation of the little one you are about to produce. Each member of the family tries to establish where they stand in relation to the baby, almost like asserting visitation rights.

Baby Byte:
There's something even bigger than the big, fat wedding. The bigger, fatter, we-have-come-to-see-the-baby thang!

But it's not just family though. Pregnancy is a social event, because everyone wants to participate, to stake their claim. And I mean everyone. That lady you sat next to in the train. The receptionist you don't know the name of, but smile at every day. The librarian in your office. The watchman. Your maid. The office boy, because his wife is pregnant too. Your friend's driver.

It looks like the universe expects you to include itself in your life, and wants you to pay it forward.

3

Have Bump. Will Flaunt.

There are two ways to look at pregnancy. One is to constantly moan that you can't get into your favourite clothes. That everything is 'too tight'. That you need to go shopping. That you have 'nothing to wear'. That you have gained 'too much weight'. That you have no control over what you eat.

The other is to celebrate the fact that you don't have to get into your thin clothes anymore. Or bother about your waistline. Or suck your stomach in.

Before maternity chic became official, women spent a large part of their pregnancy camouflaging their bump under huge tents or oversized clothes, and ended up looking like bag-ladies. Today, it's all about preg-couture, or inventing ways to highlight your new assets – your bump for sure. And most definitely your new curves, boobs, hair, skin, whatever looks better than before.

After month five, no matter what you do, the whole world knows you are pregnant anyway. So why not celebrate your bump? Which is what I did. So while I never deviated from my small size, I wore stuff that fitted well around the bust and covered, yet flaunted my bump well. Since I felt feminine and yet thought practical, I went the dresses way. Once you wear them, there is less to negotiate in terms of belts, zippers or buttons. This might seem trivial, but when you have to pee every twenty minutes, think of how much a set of fussy buttons or a belt and zipper can add to the nuisance.

There are pregnant women who make it their mission to get into their old clothes and that, to me, is a bit desperate. Because there is a difference between a pleasant bump that is shapely and gradual and an unsightly bump that is just shouting out loud, 'Gawd, I am oozing out of everything!'

Unless you have a huge case of thyroid disorder or water retention or some such, most of us have pretty much the same physique, tummy upwards and waist downwards even when pregnant. Which means – if you had good legs, you still have good legs. If your collar bones were your assets, they still are. And if you had a good décolletage, it just got better (but might soon border on the immodest).

If you want the bump to tease, not attack, avoid short tops or low-waist skirts. They can be a bit unsightly. So are clothes where the buttons threaten to pop out from over the belly. On the other hand, you don't want to waste those legs. Think medium to long stretch skirt. Think leggings that flaunt your legs and calves. Think tops that fit nicely around the chest and flounce thereon. Think slip-ons, shifts, and minimum negotiation with zippers, buttons or belts. Think comfy-sexy, not laboured-sexy.

Baby Byte:
We like to be flaunted. But please do it with taste.

This is the only period of your life when a bikini can be worn with abandon, because once the flatness of the stomach is not a prerequisite, it doesn't really matter how much of it spills out really. And to anyone giving you the look, you can shout out loud, 'I am not fat! I'm pregnant!!'

The transition from thick waist to cute bump is a cute but frustrating one. Sometimes it can take up to three to four months. At five months, the bump is eminently show-offable. Your sexuality is at its prime and this is the time to flaunt it. Time to unearth

that lycra dress you loved, but never could wear all these years, because you were never 'thin enough'. Or there was only so much stomach you could suck in. Go wear it now, no one's looking. Turn your excess baggage into an advantage.

Baby Byte:
Don't believe her when she says she only put on eight kilograms. She just stopped weighing herself after that.

If you are constantly overcome by a desire to shop for clothes during your pregnancy, here's a heads-up. The minute the 'maternity' tag is attached to an item of clothing, it comes at a premium. So improvise. The magic words are export surplus. Recycle (husband's shirts). Versatile (wrap dresses, tunics). Long-term (leggings, leggings, leggings). Of course exceptions can be made for splurging on the maternity LBD or a nice, summery brunch dress.

As for overalls, Hollywood wears them all the time, and sure they do look cute, but what do women do with their bladders, I wonder? It takes sixty seconds longer to pee when you are in that jumpsuit. When your uterus shrinks your bladder into oblivion, those sixty seconds can be agony.

Around month nine, style and elegance can take a walk. Because now, all you care about is being able to stand up every time you sit down (mostly on the pot). Or be able to sleep comfortably (the term comfort used relatively here). It's also when people around you begin to treat you like some kind of electric-shock-producing equipment (jerking away from your circumference).

I was never a fan of the salwar kameez. A drawstring mishap in the office loo made me swear off them completely. First, it's tough to determine where to wear the blessed salwar (above, below or at navel). Having done that, it has a treacherous ability to slip down at inappropriate times, or just get knotted up and refuse to unknot.

Once, as I was hurrying to pee, the drawstring of my salwar slipped back into its opening. Drat! I tried some manoeuvres of pulling it out, but since my belly got in the way, I couldn't see what I was doing. Those were the most frustrating twenty minutes of my life! Then I realised I still had my phone with me, so I called one of my colleagues. She came to the loo with a hairpin and I was rescued, and so was the drawstring.

Note to self: Unless it is a stretch churidar, don't bother with Indian wear. I still don't know how sari petticoats work in pregnancy. Do they make them elasticated?

For home-wear, once I had outgrown all my comfy T-shirts and nightwear, I found the husband's T-shirts a good place to raid. I had a huge stack of black to choose from. It was his favourite colour, although I felt weird wearing such a non-happy colour on the baby, night after night. They were super comfy though, even if inelegant, and I wore them over tracks or leggings which stretched all the way till delivery. On hot days, I lolled about in just a T-shirt.

I then went on to raid his boxers and his shirts, till he protested and asked me to please stop wearing his clothes.

Boob-side story

Soon after you cross your 'look-I-am-still-the-same-size' zone, which could take three to five months, your anatomy starts protesting. The first shrieks come from your breasts, which are obviously not too happy in the same old bras, however sexy they make you feel. Underwire, which was once the champion of the cleavage (especially for the small-busted), is now the enemy. Every time I wore one of my favourite La Senza bras, I felt breathless, almost in bondage. Sports bras were the next choice for comfort, but your breasts feel strangely vulnerable and unprotected under them.

Eventually, there comes a point when you give in to the 'support bra' – those clinically displayed, non-sexy, colourless gear ('only black and white available,' they will tell you). When you first look at them, you reel in shock. Which self-respecting woman of moderate style would wear them? They look like your grandmommy's bras, cover most of your breasts and a large part of your chest. And cleavage? What cleavage? Ergo, you feel like a nun. But, like hell, they are comfortable and make your boobs feel secure and looked after again.

Breasts also have a treacherous way of sending false alarms that they have grown when they actually haven't, so hold off on going and buying the next size. (Sometimes, you can skip the bra and wear layers, although you have to be a modest size for this.) The period of bra-size change could differ from woman to woman. For me, around six to seven months is when my breasts begged for more support. (I was a 32B graduating to a 34 C.)

If you found support bras gauche, wait till you get to the nursing bra stage. These are fitted with torture straps (or so they appear to be) in front that allow you to release your boobs, one at a time, without having to undo the bra. I thought it was too much technology for a bra, but a few months later, when I was trying to balance a baby on my boob, prop up a feeding pillow and unhook a bra at the same time in order to nurse, I was thankful. I personally found them comfortable, but opinion seems to be divided on that.

Baby Byte:
We don't care how ugly the nursing bra is, it just means less fumbling for us.

Of course, if you think nursing bras are uncool, you could wear layers of T-shirts or singlets, but we still live in a tropical country. How much clothing can you handle? Besides, what will you do about leakage? You don't want to be walking around with two wet patches where your boobs are, do you? The thing about a nursing bra is that it's designed to accommodate the breast pad, that absorber of your overflow, that saviour of your dignity, that leak-guard of your over-lactating (in some cases) breasts post baby.

Unfortunately, not much work or research has been done in the panty area. Thongs and bikini-cut panties, which usually work well when visible panty line is a concern, now feel inordinately intrusive and offer no coverage at all. If there was a panty equivalent for a sports bra, that would be the one to buy, but there isn't. Maternity panties are yet to be invented in India and I didn't see the point of spending a fortune on gauche underwear. I personally found my husband's boxers perfect for the night, but for the day you need something more snug and secure, something that covers at least some of your belly nicely. For lack of anything else, the mommy panties you wear during your period do manage to provide decent cover. Else look for ones with legs, even bloomers will do.

One highly overrated and much-marketed item in maternity wear is the discreet nursing top. A dichotomy, to say the least. When my friend Rashmi was visiting from Hong Kong and asked me what I wanted, I said 'nursing tops' since the ones I saw here cost more than a dress. She got me two, of which one looked like the blouse equivalent of a wrap dress, with flaps to pop the boobs out, and was very snug. But it had so much cleavage potential (it barely escaped the areola) that it hardly fitted the discreet bill. The other looked like it was some sort of heavy-duty combat gear with suspicious holes hidden within two layers of fabric, and they had to be correctly positioned to be unravelled for the baby's suckling. Whenever I wore it, I felt like a terrorist hiding a bomb.

I'm Pregnant, Not Terminally Ill, You Idiot!

I realised later that there is no such thing as discreet nursing and I shouldn't have bothered with suitable gear at all. My baby used to flail his arms in glee, unhinging any fabric that came his way. He also produced guttural, near-orgasmic sounds while nursing, so it was like a public announcement anyway. I saw no point having to negotiate through a complicated top to get to the act. Breastfeeding babies are notorious for exposing you in the most inappropriate of places. If they let you throw a stole or a shawl over to cover yourself, be grateful. I have had several wardrobe malfunctions and learnt to see the humour in it.

In the end, the best maternity or mommy-wear is one that you feel comfortable in, whatever the label may say. So if you can wear what you always wore and get on with it, why not? As for nursing ponchos, they look ridiculous, even if they are designed by Rohit Bal.

4

That's My Bump. Talk to ME!

The first three months of being pregnant are like having a secret and feeling burdened by it. Here's the logic – information to be shared on a need-to-know basis. Plus there is the added anxiety of the first three months being the most fragile. Sixty percent of women are known to miscarry in the first trimester, so it's all about being absolutely sure everything is okay before you announce to the world. In any case, why tell until you show?

Of course the mothers and the aunts will over-obsess about the evil eye. 'You don't know what goes on in people's minds. It is inauspicious to tell before the fourth month.'

The evil eye is also a ploy used by the older generation to force rest upon the newly pregnant woman. According to my encyclopaedic aunt, 'If you tell the woman to rest and not jump or travel or move around too much in the first three months because it could harm the foetus, she might act defiant. But telling her that it will "ward off the evil eye" might do the trick.' She believes it's easier to get people to obey a religious or superstitious diktat than a scientific one. Perhaps she is right. Pregnancy does make you somewhat irrational. At least it did me.

It is ironic though, that the minute you know you are pregnant, you start making changes to your life. Some subtle, some not so subtle. So smokers stop smoking, gymmers stop gymming, drinkers stop drinking, runners stop running. Now, this is in full public view, so it's hard to explain the change without actually giving the reason for it. Something's gotta give, right?

Let's say you manage to go about pretending things are just the same and act breezy till you show. But your body is doing a different number – you may have morning sickness, afternoon sickness, late evening sickness or even an all-day sickness. The wooziness and lethargy can be hard to camouflage, even if you are a M.A.C. concealer goddess.

I had it relatively good, with just a slow-motion-in-the-afternoon sickness, a feeling of ravenousness every two hours (and hence a need to carry multiple food boxes) and a craving for citrus fruit. This was not tough to explain as I have always been a mid-meal snacker and fruit chomper. People just thought I was being my usual, 'where-does-all-that-food-go' self. Since I never threw up during my pregnancy, there was none of those aunty metaphors shouting, 'Good news?'

But here's the painful part: Every time you refuse a glass of wine or a cocktail, you need a story ready.

'Not drinking?'

'Not really, no.'

'You mean like, "not drinking" not drinking?'

'Yup, that's right.'

'Can't imagine you without a drink. How can you not drink at Becky's wedding?'

'Actually, I'm on antibiotics.'

'It's okay, just skip one dose. They say the body takes less time to process alcohol than medicine.'

'I don't feel like it, really!'

'Whatever.'

I found out I was pregnant two weeks before my friend Becky got married. The wedding was a total alcohol-fuelled party heaven, with hen nights, cocktails, dances, drinks, pre- and post-parties at the drop of a hat. The whole world was invited. There was no way I could not go, as both she and her fiancé Ashwin were really close friends. But how to camouflage the off-alcohol thing? I realised I would lose my mind explaining to everyone. So I diligently nursed a glass of lemonade with ice through the shindig, pretending it was vodka tonic. Dee always made sure the glass was full. No one asked any more questions. As for the ceremonial glass of wine, well, I just emptied it into the grass when no one was looking. In any case, people were too drunk to be bothered.

But there was the need to eat every half hour. I couldn't even sit through the wedding vows without needing a snack. I had snuck in plenty of granola bars in my purse, which helped me while I waited for real food to show up.

I don't know how I did it, but I pulled off an entire alcohol-infused wedding with almost zero alcohol. The only event I skipped was the hen night. Somehow, the thought of male strippers and wild dancing all night with a bunch of drunken women made me retch. I was the new Cinderella. I had to be in bed by midnight.

Baby Byte:
Don't believe her when she says she never had any alcohol. Some nights, I just forgot to kick and I know what that was a result of.

My friend Parisha used the euphemism 'I had a really big night yesterday' in the initial months whenever she had to exercise the 'not drinking' clause among friends. Later, when the secret was out, they got back at her. 'Big night, huh?'

In a few weeks, you become good at faking normalcy. And just when you think you have it, pat! Your game is busted. When I was around eight weeks pregnant, Dee and I were at a brunch which had a complimentary Thai foot spa. I decided to indulge. A little pampering was in order, I thought. The guy in charge asked me, 'Are you pregnant?'

This was a first. I had dressed carefully, so there was no question of the bump showing. How did he know?

I pretended to be affronted. Is that how people talked to fat women?

'Why? Why do you ask?'

'Ma'am, I don't mean to be intrusive, but the regular foot-massage techniques could be harmful to pregnant women. Some of the pressure points are over-sensitive. I am sorry, but it's our policy to ask everyone to be safe.'

I looked around. No one I knew was listening.

'Errr...I'll come back later.'

I disappeared from the scene.

There are many such giveaway moments. Refusing to donate blood. Refusing to watch a violent film. Refusing to go river-rafting with your bunch of friends, pretending there is too much on your plate. Refusing all-nighter clubbing escapades. Feeling a slight trepidation going through an X-ray machine in a mall. Having the jitters taking an autorickshaw when you are in a no-cab zone and you and your photographer colleague just have to get to that celeb interview on time.

At the end of month three, Dee and I finally broke it to our friends one night at Blue Frog, one of the regular haunts of our gang. There was much cheering and jubilation. For the first time, I wore a bump-flaunting dress. Trisha, who was twenty-four and our youngest friend in the group, came up to me and said, 'OMG!! And I thought it would be rude to ask if you had put on weight!'

It felt like freedom. Freedom to flaunt the bump, freedom to eat like you were eating for four, freedom to excuse yourself from anything and everything, freedom to leave whenever you wished to, sleep whenever and wherever you wanted to, freedom to put your feet up, wear flats, keds or break lines in loos.

Initially, it's all fun. But soon, you will begin to realise that

you were better off with the secret. Because now, it's no longer about you – it's all about the bump. Your pregnancy is now for public consumption. If you have been a largely private person who doesn't always look for attention or approval, you might find the fuss claustrophobic. And it's nothing you can be coy or cryptic about, because, now it's all out there and everyone seems to have a Right to Information. Everyone feels something about the pregnant woman – it could be faint amusement, awe, affection, disdain, envy, or just curiosity.

The belly is now another entity, quite separate from you, but generally the object of attention or discussion. So you could be 'really big' or 'hardly showing' and you know what they are talking about.

Somewhere in the fifth or sixth month of your pregnancy, you stop existing. It is as though you might as well have been somewhere else, or had an out-of-body experience of sorts because no one really cares about you. They are all talking to the bump. It's as though you are your bump, and that's all the identity you have. Nothing is about you anymore, what you think, what you feel, who you are. Some of them don't even have a real conversation with you. They look at you, look at the bump, look at you again as if to say, 'Is that what I think it is?'

Baby Byte:
I know it's all about me, but please don't ignore her. She is my chief food source, at least for a while.

Once you get used to pregnancy lingo, it's more of the same.
    She: (pointing to bump) Are you…?
    You: Yes.

She: *(still pointing to bump)* How many months?
You: Twenty-six weeks.
She: *(slightly foxed)* That's err...six months?
You: It's twenty-six weeks.
She: Oh!
Point understood.

And if you do something out of character in your new avatar, like use swear words or randomly start shaking a leg at an office party, or have a glass of wine or jump into the pool, you will be treated as some sort of weirdo.

'Is it okay for the baby?'

Suddenly, no one is discussing sexual politics with you, or relationship blues, or office romances or even dating dynamics. You are out of the radar, off-limits, almost holier than thou. Even your best friends have stopped talking to you about stuff you used to talk about. All they are interested in is: 'How does it feel? Is it kicking?'

Baby Byte:
So what if I'm still inside? I have a life too.

Of course, good things happen too. You have random niceties happening at work. People are opening doors for you. People stop smoking around you. Office boy brings you tea before you ask for it. Exactly the way you want it. People who never smiled at you before in corridors begin to smile.

More questions will continue in the months to follow, depending on the degree of familiarity.

'So, is the baby kicking yet?'
'How do you know if the baby is sleeping or awake?'

'Is it true that you can sense the baby eating your food?'
'Can you tell where the head is and where the legs are?'
'Does the baby punch too?'
'Can it smile? Laugh?'
'Does it have hair yet?'
'Will you let me touch you when it kicks?'
'How does the baby pee? Poo?'

Baby Byte:
Stop embarrassing her with such personal questions. She is as clueless as you are.

The women who've been-there-done-that are usually more clinical:
'Who is your ob-gyn? Which hospital?'
'How's the blood-work? All good?'
'Any thyroid? Water retention? Acidity? Gestational diabetes?'
'Have you had your nuchal scan yet? What about Triple Marker? Anomaly? Bart? Are you doing an amnio?'
'How many sonographies so far?'
'Any placenta previa?'
'No bed rest, I hope?'
'What about pigmentation?'
'Has it engaged?'
'Are you doing Kegels?'

Then there is always much ado about the kick. It is something that is savoured with equal delight by all – the rookies and the seasoned. Somehow the thought of one human being occupying the insides of another human being and kicking the host in defiance seems funny and delightful to most. I have had people wanting to experience it firsthand and offering to put their ears or heads or hands on my belly just to feel the kicks. It sure is the funniest bit about pregnancy – something that still lingers in memory.

More things happen after the bump. You are exempted from X-ray machine scans at airports and other places and can officially break queues. People about to board elevators, stop when they know you are there. People at malls become a little more respectful when you are getting on or off elevators. Sometimes queues at supermarkets seem to shrink too. I guess it is more out of awkwardness. People treat a pregnant woman like she's nude or something. Like they don't know what is the appropriate thing to do. Of course there will always be the eager salesperson who will try to sell you diapers, or stem cell banking or offer you a deal on baby products or child-savings plans or membership to a toy library.

But somehow your bump doesn't really cut much ice with public transport for some reason, or even something as innocuous as hailing a cab. Or getting a cabbie to drive at a speed that could, at best, not kill anyone. Especially you or the baby.

Public engagement with your bump gets worse as the months progress. First everyone and their mothers-in-law wants to predict the sex of the baby. Mine took a look at me and said, 'It's a boy.' I was stumped. We were rooting for a girl all along and always referred to the baby as a *she*.

Then my friend Tarana made me do a full turnaround, took a good hard look at my bump, my breasts and my bum and declared, 'No way is it a girl!'

'How do you know?' I asked her.

'Well, your bum is not spilling out, neither is your face or your arms. It's a boy!'

I don't know if it was all their collective will, but it turned out to be a boy in the end.

Baby Byte:
It's so embarrassing. They are talking about my sex. Should I protest?

Around month nine, the emotions of fellow human beings change to fear and panic, especially if your bump is huge in comparison to you (like mine was), and arrives before you in the room. All they are thinking is: What if she goes into labour while at work? What if her water breaks? What if she slips in the office when the corridor is being cleaned? What are we supposed to do? My yoga buddy Vankan would run miles away from me if I ever happened to sit next to him in class on my mat. 'God, you make me nervous. What if you fall on me?'

It suddenly seems too much responsibility. People would secretly not want to be around you and are waiting for the day when you actually go on maternity leave. Because now, they have all had enough of the bump. All they want is for you to get out of their sight.

Baby Byte:
Stop being so paranoid. I am just a baby, not a bomb!

5
Thinking Good Thoughts — My Foot!

It's a truth universally acknowledged that motherhood might be a chance to reconstruct yourself. Naomi Wolf, in her book *Misconceptions* says:

> But pregnancy, on the other hand – like, perhaps, a terminal illness or a state of grace – seemed to make that barrier between the fretful, mundane, everyday world and the luminous 'ground of being' that much thinner. It seemed to efface that barrier, thinning it to transparency. I did not imagine that pregnant women were 'naturally' any more sensitive or exalted than people in any other condition; only it seemed as if – perhaps only because we are in such a twilight state, a melting down and reconstituting of the self – there was more opportunity to hear strains from what must be the other side, the moral music of the sphere.

Motherhood is supposed to bless you with this new aura, this general state of well-being – something that will neutralise all the negativity around and inside you; something that will make bad energy go away and good energy stay. Fine. Great. If you are planning on an image makeover, this would be a good place to start.

'Babies,' Wolf speculates, 'in that peculiar mystical state, are sort of leaky little understudies for God. With each baby the human species gets a chance to break out of the self into the service of something so "other" that the reasons for conditional love can give way to faith in unconditional love.'

My very spiritual sister noticed I had become a calmer person post giving birth. My mother felt I listened better and was less critical of her opinions. My friend Rama thought I had become more tolerant and forgiving of people. Most friends were shocked that I was such a natural at being a mom. It didn't say much about my earlier avatar for sure.

I used to write a gender column called *Chickwit* for the *Hindustan Times*, which, more often than not, was a wicked take on relationships, dating and sexual politics, men and their idiocies. Post baby, the no-holds barred, incisive bitchiness, which worked really well for the column went missing for a while. One loyal reader, Biren, wrote to me: 'I can't deal with this mellowness. Where is the mean you? I need to read wicked stuff in the mornings, not feel-good stuff.'

I promised him it was a phase and my fangs would return. They did. But it hasn't been the same. I still get accused of mellow.

Baby Byte:
Mommies are great at faking the beatific look. But only I know what she looks like when she's alone.

When you are pregnant, people expect you to turn into this goddess who is a temple of calm, doesn't display negative emotions, like anger, jealousy or bitchiness, doesn't use swear words (what if the baby picks them up?) and in general, is smiling and cheerful all the time. That, to me is the most frustrating part of pregnancy. Yes, the good hormones do ward off the bad energy, but there are bad days for everyone. And sometimes, you lose it.

Rashi, who had a four-year-old when I was pregnant, told me I should get a new vocabulary. 'The last time you were here, my daughter picked up s**t!'

There goes my power of speech, I thought. I may as well enrol for Vipassana and stay there until the baby is born.

Whenever I lost my cool or used a four-letter word or did something equally abominable in my mother's view, she told me, 'Be careful. The baby is listening.'

My point was, yes, but if I don't let off steam, the baby will be listening to all my repressed anger, and that might be worse.

In short, nothing in your life has changed, except that there is a spectator inside you who is taking it all in. The only way you can become the epitome of calm is if you stop going to work, travelling anywhere, talking to anyone, and just staying put and listening to Bach at home. Sure, there were fleeting moments of peace and quiet, when the husband would indulge me with his famous calf massage, pour me an occasional glass of wine or beer (yes!), and we would talk to the baby in dulcet tones. It felt like this was the best time of my life and I had never been so tranquil or centred before.

Till I went to work the next day. And found that life and the universe around me was pretty much the same as before. People were still being mean to animals. Trees were still being cut randomly. Drivers were still driving with their eyes shut and their brains locked up somewhere. Rich brats in posh cars were still pretending that a pothole-laden road was the expressway. Colleagues were still slacking off. Telemarketing pests and PR executives were still calling you at 2 p.m. Stock broking companies were still bulk-texting me hot tips at 6 a.m. My mother was still whining about my father.

In the midst of all this, you are expected to be this immaculate, calm mother who will give birth to this angel of a baby who will do everything right, stay happy, never cry and always sleep when you want it to. Such babies and mothers don't exist and the sooner you learn that, the better it is for you. I found that when I came

I'm Pregnant, Not Terminally Ill, You Idiot!

to terms with my imperfections instead of trying to fight them, I was able to be a much better mother.

Yes, thinking good thoughts, listening to 'good music' and reading 'good books' and looking at pretty things is a recipe for a happy pregnancy, but how easy is it to see it through really?

And then there are the pregnophobes (read people who hate you because you are pregnant). So cynical singletons and man-haters now hate you even more because you are an affirmation of womanhood. Your GBF (gay best friend) now realises that the womb will be a permanent wall between you and him. Procreation is something that will never figure in his life. Maternity leave will never be in his list of company benefits.

Baby haters – men and women, who believe having a child is ensnaring to their freedom and their rocking life – will now look at you with more suspicion. Peers who were married much before you and haven't had success in the baby-making department will now get all competitive.

A pregnant woman signifies different things to different people. At the very basic level – a marriage, a man, and sex. At a deeper level – permanence, continuum, hope, dreams. So the way you perceive a pregnant woman boils down to what your aspirations are, how you see yourself a few years from now, what is your relationship stage, what you expect from a man/relationship, how much of it is coming true. Somehow, coming face to face or being in close proximity with a pregnant woman fast-forwards your thinking to a large extent about such things. It highlights why your life is not moving in that direction. So you end up hating the pregnant woman for having what you don't have.

With such negativity around, it is not the easiest thing to be a nice person when you are pregnant. And then the whole world begins to bombard you with advice, which makes it even worse. Yes, the hormones are supposed to be doing their work and making you feel all maternal and nesting, someone who is the epitome of zen.

But even after the unease of the first trimester has settled down and your feel-good phase is about to begin, you will still find yourself rattled every once in a while. Husbands are easy targets for steam-letting. One night, I was feeling particularly restless and the husband still hadn't come to bed. I stormed into his room (aptly called the gaming room). 'Why aren't you in bed yet? It's 2 a.m.!'

'Err...I was just trying to finish a level (gaming lingo, which means kill some people, loot and plunder some). I promise I will be in bed in half-an-hour.'

I piped up.

'Why do you have to game every night? Can't you see I can't sleep, lying in bed, my insides being kicked royally? On top of that, I am wondering if you have eaten? Or if you are drinking too much? Or if you have fallen asleep on the couch?'

'Babe, I am gaming in my own house, not downing tequila shots with random party animals.'

'You think you are doing me a favour?'

'What do you want me to do?'

'Please turn this off. It is really violent. Will you keep gaming when the baby arrives too?'

I started bawling.

He is nervous by now, and puts the controller down.

'Can I get you something? Herbal tea? Nimboo pani? Juice?'

'No, my calves hurt.'

'Okay, will give you a good massage.'

And he does.

If that was not enough, your mother is now calling you four times a day instead of two.

'Have you eaten?'

'No, Mom, I will now.'

'What? Not eaten? It's one o'clock!'

'I know, Mom. I was busy at work.'

'My god! Why don't they understand that you are pregnant and you need to eat on time?'

Baby Byte:
O gawd, it must be one of those phone calls. She's been sulking for an hour and I haven't even been fed!

It doesn't end. The mother-in-law, shortly after whining about her driver, will have her two-bits to add. 'I hope you are relaxing, thinking nice thoughts. You must look at beautiful things, baby pictures in books. It's good for the baby.'

It's not difficult to figure why you need to let off steam. Pregnancy mood swings are like PMT – writ large, and last much longer. The heavier you get, the lower your threshold gets. And then, nothing goes your way. You want to sleep. Baby doesn't. You want to have sex. Husband doesn't. You want to fart. You can't, because you are in a goddamn meeting. And then the world tells you. Think. Good. Thoughts.

So what do you do to feel better? Shopping may not be the greatest thing because you have no energy or patience to try on stuff. Meditation is not for you. Going for a walk has its own problems. Movies? Well, where will you leave your bladder? Eating? Well, how much can you eat really?

So you bark some more. At someone. Anyone.

I would leave my home for work every morning feeling all positive, chirpy, full of happy thoughts, in tune with my inner goddess. But by the time I got to the office, after the hour's commute, I would be snarling, thanks to potholes, lane changers, and inveterate honkers. I realised that the more you focus on thinking happy thoughts, the more angry thoughts you can think of.

The last trimester is a true test of your Zen state, if ever there was a fleeting one. It's when you walk around all the time feeling your bladder is going to burst, although you had just emptied it five minutes ago. Or you feel like your spinal cord is going to lose its way into a place of unknown destination. And your baby wants you to keep on moving and kicks you nineteen to a dozen every time you sit down. Or when you are just about to break wind in the office aisle and the new cute guy decides to emerge out of nowhere, flashing his cutest smile.

Baby Byte:
So what if she's a mommy?
She has hormones too! Lots of them actually.

To top it all, your doctor treats you like you had an illness and robotically asks questions like:

'Is there pain? Spotting? Nausea? Sensitivity?'

'No.'

'Okay. Everything is fine. But no high heels, perfume, tight clothes, nail polish, alcohol or cigarettes. And no keeping relations with husband (he means sex here).'

Now, how does one have happy thoughts? I tried though. I got myself a driver. I thought half my anger was related to road-rage, and if I manage that, I can be the beautiful person pregnancy made me. Within a week, I realised it was a wrong call.

One day, after his sixth offence in the one-hour ride, I told him I had enough and it was either my way or no way. He told me he was sick of my mood swings and my mouthing off to him every day. That did it. I asked him to stop the car in the middle of the road. 'Please leave right now. I'll take it from here. Come to my office to collect your salary.'

He said, 'Okay, give it to me now.'

I found myself get angrier and angrier. I asked him to drive me to the nearest ATM, where I gave him his money, drove myself to work, and sat down at my desk, my heart beating at two hundred per minute, my baby all quiet, wondering what pissed off mommy so much.

Baby Byte:
When the fuck is she going to calm down?
I need to sleep.

I got back to driving, being blunt, and irreverent. Not necessarily in that order. Yes, my ugly side raised its head once in a while and let out the monster, but it kept my happy side safe. I also sacked my holier-than-thou doctor and got myself a new one who made me laugh. It meant more commute, but I couldn't be bothered. I was becoming an expert at bladder management.

I guess throughout pregnancy there are so many people inhabiting your universe that by the end of it, you just want to turn into a recluse. The nicer term for it is nesting, I think. Towards the end of my pregnancy, I just wanted to be all by myself on an island. Perhaps with my mother, who would look after me and feed me. And the husband who would drive me around and massage my calves.

Once the baby pops out, being nice (to anyone other than the baby) gets progressively harder. I used to have screaming matches with my mother every other day and the poor soul still stood by me for six months.

'I think you should rest.'

'I know, Amma. I will.'

'Why don't you sleep now? He (the baby) is sleeping peacefully.'

'But I am not feeling sleepy now. And it's 11 a.m., for god's sake!'

'Maybe if you stop staring at the computer, you might. How many times have I told you it is not good?'

'WHAT? WHAT DO YOU MEAN? AM I JUST A MILKING COW? I HAVE A MIND, YOU KNOW!'

'Please don't shout. The baby will hear you. Alright, if you don't want to sleep, don't sleep. I am just concerned about you.'

'Then don't be.'

And just when you think it can't get any worse, it does. In fact I regressed from nice to not-so-nice to downright witch by the time the baby was six months old. Either it was the cook or the cleaning lady or the numerous twits who showed up for nanny jobs or the DSAs who called you at 2 p.m., or the grocer who sent you a wrong delivery or the census guy who was just doing a population count or the new tout who wanted to sell you a broadband plan or just about anyone.

Yes, the hormones are to blame. They play games with your neurotransmitter levels and make them run amuck. Psychoanalysts also point out other causes for the moody blues – changes in family dynamics, anxiety about life changes, fear of loss of control, recuperating body, changes in metabolism, added financial stress, and a huge desire to be the best parent. The bottom line is, it messes you up. Seriously.

I look at it this way. You can either be the nice girl, take everything in your stride, find your life being dictated by family and other animals, and be told what to do and what not to do. Or you can take a stand and be an 'I-will-do-exactly-as-I-please-thank-you' kind of girl. The former is a sure recipe for prolonged postpartum depression. The latter may make you unpopular, but keep you happier and most definitely, saner.

6

Sneezy, Sleepy, Woozy, Weepy, Grumpy, Happy and Farty

It is a huge relief when your pregnancy begins to show. Really. Till then, you feel like a bit of a klutz. Your breasts are feeling weird and sore. You feel breathless in your bra. You need to eat something, anything, all the time. Your favourite skinny jeans don't feel right anymore. Your selection of footwear is getting all modest, because you are too woozy for heels most of the time.

Your body on the other hand seems to say, 'Nothing to declare!' So basically, you can't break lines, no one offers you a seat, no one says sorry if they accidentally brush against you in a crowd, no one understands why you suddenly have mood swings, no one gets why you *have* to eat.

So one part of you wants to explain and shout from the rooftops that you are pregnant. The saner half is trying to smile through all the unease and lethargy and abnormal appetite, pretending everything is normal. Those twelve-fourteen weeks seem like the longest waiting period ever.

As to what's happening in your mind, well, mood swings are perhaps just one of the most underrated things about pregnancy. Everyone has them, whatever else they might tell you. Some are over with it in the first trimester. Some are not hit by it till the last. But sooner or later, the moody hormones are bound to strike. You are prone to feel depressed, suffer low self-esteem, have anxiety attacks, feel lonely, weepy, etc.

My friend Shilpa used to be weepy all the time in her first trimester. 'It took hardly anything to trigger off a flood of tears. A movie, a visual of a child crying and that was it. I would bawl and bawl,' she said.

As for me, I remember feeling very depressed when the 26/11 terror attacks happened. I was just a few weeks pregnant and wondered, *what world was I bringing a child into?*

But strange things happen to your body and bodily functions when you are pregnant. No one talks about them, as some of them are quite un-ladylike, but they have happened to all. Even to Victoria Beckham.

One common phenomenon is water retention. It could either be genuine (a thyroid malfunction), or an excuse for putting on more weight than is normally prescribed. So your whole body, especially the extremities, and sadly, your face look all puffed up. Sometimes, you might have to put your feet up, lest they swell like a balloon. Shoe sizes are difficult to figure at this point, so you regress to wearing adjustable granny sandals or moccasins you can squeeze into. My friend Sheetal would swell up at her feet every time she sat down, and then couldn't get into her footwear till we massaged her feet for a good half hour.

Baby Byte:
Don't believe this water retention rubbish. She's just been over-eating and trying to cover up.

Other things may wave the pregnancy flag. Your hair may act virulent. If it's curly, it may want to get straight, and if it's straight, it may develop obstinate waves. You may have teeth and gum issues: like bleeding, sensitivity (calcium, your ob-gyn will be quick to point). You may also have sneezing fits or your nose may leak randomly, due to increased pressure in your capillaries thanks to all those pregnancy hormones. Basically, all the loose ends of your body will protest a wee bit till they come to terms with the whole baby thing.

I'm Pregnant, Not Terminally Ill, You Idiot!

One thing you keep waiting for (although people assure you it is here) is the pregnancy glow. If there ever was a pregnancy cliché, this is one. We all have heard of the 'radiant' pregnant woman, but how many of you have actually seen her? Most of the time, you are busy wilting away in air-conditioning or pollution, dying for your skin to hydrate, so even if the glow appeared, it has made a quick exit.

Although there is a fleeting period, somewhere between month four and month seven, that you seem bouncier than usual and perhaps the positive energy or the good hormones reflect on your face. There. That's the pregnancy glow. Enjoy it. Capture it. Document it. It will not last very long. But for the most part, when people say you are glowing, they are just being nice, or you are just shiny from over-moisturising to counter the wilting.

Basically the hormone overdrive shows on your skin, so if you had acne or blemishes, they miraculously disappear like in those ads on television, which feature a distressed teenager before and after she applies some guck. On the other hand, if it was clear, you might suddenly be ridden with freckles and a few warts for good measure. Also, they are not restricted to the face and decide to travel to your neck and back and other unmentionable places as well. Some of you might develop an overall tan and appear like you just returned from the beach. My friend Anu had an overactive case of pigmentation and by the end, looked like she'd acquired a deep Goa tan, which added far more oomph to her look. She never did get the pregnancy glow, but got far more brownie points for her tan.

Glow or no glow, by the second trimester, your body is flush with the good hormones and you are still not 'that heavy' to feel tired all the time, so you can make the most of it. You wear your pretty dresses. You are at your sexy best. You tilt your head and laugh when you have that elegant glass of wine. You have doors opened for you all the time. Men are still flirting with you. Women are still in awe of you. Even David Beckham said that his wife was at her sexiest when she was pregnant.

Another thing that you will deal with great nonchalance during pregnancy is bodily fluids and sounds. Breaking wind after the first few months will be second nature, and don't believe anyone who pretends they don't know what you are talking about. It happened to me in the most inappropriate places like office corridors. Yes, you are usually on your way to the loo to be discreet when it happens, but sometimes, it just gets the better of you.

I used to break wind in my sleep all the time, and the husband would wake up and say, 'Oh, we are so married.' And I would retort, 'Oh, I am so pregnant!'

Breaking wind is second nature to a pregnant woman. What else would you expect if you are diligent about following that healthy, high-fibre diet? Perhaps the body gets a bit of a shock trying to metabolise all that you eat and it is its way of protesting or letting you know to take it easy. It happens to all of us. It has happened to Angelina Jolie, too, and every Brad Pitt has to deal with it. If you consider how much baby farting you are going to have to deal with, this is nothing.

Baby Byte:
Wait till I'm out, and I'll teach her what it is to be woken up by farts!

Next in the pregnancy sound-effects department is burping. In which, post every meal, you produce not-so musical sounds, which are hard to decode – sometimes, they fall in between a burp and a hiccup. Sometimes the baby hiccups too, and if you are around a pregnant belly, it can be a fun experience to feel/hear. It can also be a pleasant distraction (and an excuse) for your own hiccups.

By the seventh month, you wish they made pregnancy diapers. Yes, now the pee runneth over every once in a while, especially when you are laughing, sneezing or using more oxygen than normal. Your bladder is getting pushed into a corner as your uterus enlarges with the baby inside. The bad word is incontinence. They say your sphincter muscles get confused (whatever!). When it first happened to me, I was a little embarrassed and by then, I had stopped reading those pregnancy books. I had no clue till I got talking to Preeta.

'Did you feel like peeing all the time?'

'You know what? I could well have worn diapers. I was peeing even when I was not peeing.'

'You mean like...?'

'You got it.'

And that was that. Sorted. I was not abnormal. It happened to everyone. Good.

Once I was at a stand-up comedy night, and I laughed so much, I had to excuse myself. I had a ready retort if the guy had to heckle me. 'You are so funny, I peed in my pants!' I think wisdom prevailed and he didn't.

As the pregnancy progresses, you raise the bar as far as sound effects go. By month eight, it is about who can snore the loudest, you or the husband. And don't tell me you don't snore. I asked your husband.

But that's not the worst thing that can happen to you. The worst is to be hit by an all-time libido high and have no one to have sex with. Husbands don't help much (mine was too afraid of hurting the baby) and are busy hiding for cover at least in the later months, so you might be better off with your vibrator.

And some dumb books scare you by saying that orgasms might preempt labour. So you feel horny all the time and desperately want to do wild things to the cute trainee in the office who is fifteen years younger than you and is even afraid to make eye contact. But your morality is at an all-time high, so you don't do any of that. Instead, you dutifully come back to your husband and plead, once more.

'Are we going to have sex?'
'Not tonight, baby, I have had a torrid day.'
'Don't lie. You are just afraid.'
'Well, yes, it feels weird.'
'Why, because of my belly?'
'No, because I feel as though I am about to have sex with my child.'

I felt like Rachel from F.R.I.E.N.D.S. Actually, worse. At least she didn't have a husband and so was free to sleep with anyone.

Baby Byte:
I have a suggestion for a baby shower gift.
Giggolo vouchers!

To add salt to the wound, your vagina seems to be on an overdrive as far as the juices go, even though it's not getting much action. The secretions might actually be overwhelming for the absorption power of your modest panties, so panty-liners will be your new best friend for this period (as will nursing bras be post baby).

And finally, the boobs.

As if in celebration of your new-found sex drive, your boobs become bigger, better, shapelier and fill into all your clothes nicely and make for great décolletage. You may increase a cup size (yay!) and a rib size (not so yay!).

For those of you, who, like me, have always been small-breasted and a 32 B was some sort of milestone in your life, there's plenty of breast coming your way. Enjoy it while it lasts. Initially, when your bra gets tighter, you wonder if your bra size could have actually increased or are you just feeling breathless because of the hormone overdrive. But since you have always been a lady of modest boobs, you act conservative and don't go out and buy the next size. Till you get to that point when your breasts are almost spilling out even on the last hook and then you know. You've got boobs. And they are here to stay. For a while, at least.

Food is always on your mind, unless you are one of those unfortunate few who can't keep anything down, even water. I never had a panipuri or gulab jamun craving at 2 a.m., like some women do. All I had was a thing for citrus fruit (it kept the nausea at bay) and a renewed interest in ice cream. Otherwise I ate like I always did, which was for three.

Once, out of curiosity, I went through a recommended nutrition chart in a 'pregnancy book' and realised that if I had to eat what they asked me to eat, I would have to be at exotic supermarkets every other day or just move to another country. So I decided to chuck the book and follow my body.

My biggest challenge was how to pack at least six small meals (and each of them fun) into my lunch bag every day, and how to make them as varied as possible, since I love to eat. The flipside was, my single biggest preoccupation while setting out for work was food. I was the certified food slut in the office.

Somewhere around month seven or eight, your centre of gravity shifts. Significantly. Despite the fact that your lunch boxes have reduced in weight now. Sometimes you have to determine whether you are walking forwards or backwards. Or whether you are walking or waddling. Can you see your toes? Yes? Then there's still a long way to go. And then you wait. And wait. And wait.

Baby Byte:
Yes, I am as bored as she is, but what to do?
We are on hold!

7
The Pregnancy Fellowship Programme

Pregnant women are free targets. Almost anyone feels free to probe, ask intimate questions, make tactless observations, bombard you with useless information and trivia. It's as though you are holding a placard that says: *Will take advice. Anytime. Any kind.* Privacy is highly overrated, more so in the Indian context. For instance, it is not considered rude to ask a newly married couple, 'Any good news?' or 'Are you planning a baby?'. So, investigating a bump is hardly perceived as rude.

Somehow, everyone – known, unknown, related, not-related – feels the need to dispense pregnancy and baby advice – and it's always free and in abundance. I guess it is a time when all hierarchies are dissolved, all sense of propriety is lost, all respect for your privacy is disregarded. Anyone who can see the bump is free to make a point.

Baby Byte:
Okay, I'm a person and so is she, so watch it! Stop objectifying us!

You can do one of two things: either react to each one and work your blood pressure up, which may not be good for you or the baby. Or, as they say, 'In one ear, out the other,' while smiling through it all.

Initially, the questioning is simpler. 'Are you taking folic acid? Calcium? Iron? Vitamins?'

If you answer yes, you will be reminded of something else that you are not taking. If you answer no, get ready to be bombarded with the dangers of not taking it.

Then there is of course the tiresome ordeal of: 'How many months? Who is the doctor? Is the baby kicking? When are you going on leave? Do you know if it's a boy or girl?'

Sometime during my eighth month, a colleague one day looked at me in shock and screamed, 'You are still here?!'

'Yes, I have two more months to go.'

'Really? You look like you could give birth any minute!'

I felt like saying, 'Yes, I feel like doing that right now and asking you to cut my umbilical cord.'

But I didn't. I was trying hard to think happy thoughts and forget the imbecile.

Of course you can't expect everyone to remember when you are due, but the repeated reminders of it are totally unnecessary (when you gotta go, you will go). Some morons might ask you if you are going to have a 'normal' delivery, like you have a penchant for paranormal activity.

At the top of the let-me-give-you-some-advice list is the mother and the mother-in-law. Then come the aunts, cousins who've been there, done that, work colleagues and then the foster mothers (usually friends). Every pregnant woman always has one friend who has been there just a wee bit before her and wants to adopt her, tell her what to do and what not to do, what to eat, what not to, what to pack in the hospital bag, the works. It's almost like you enrolled for a pregnancy fellowship programme.

'Have coconut water every day. It's good for the baby's hair,' said Parul.

I could have argued that my family was a tropical evergreen forest as far as hair was concerned. Hair was a given for my baby, unless I married someone extremely bald, which I hadn't.

'Almonds and walnuts. Great for the baby's brain,' said Suman.

'Beer. Great for the baby's skin,' said Alisha.

'Listen to Beethoven,' said Chetan. 'It will improve your child's mathematical ability. Children who are exposed to western classical music in the womb grow up to be mathematical geniuses.'

Now, I like math, and was good at it, and so, it wouldn't hurt for my child to be good at it too. But with due respect, I wasn't in the mood for Beethoven during my pregnancy. It just made me sad. So Raghu Dixit and Kannada pop it was. About the math, we'll see.

Baby Byte:
Thank god she didn't overdose me with Beethoven. Who needs math? That Dixit guy was quite a bloke. I am sure most of my kicks were courtesy him.

When the baby arrives, advice goes through the roof. Suddenly, the list of people on your advisory board grows exponentially. Every window of opportunity is exploited to overload you with advice. Mostly useless. Here are a few scenarios:

Scenario 1: You are struggling to get your maternity leave extended.

'My daughter-in-law had six months. And her company paid for everything.'

'Oh great, that's nice.'

'Why don't you just tell them you want six months off? You are in such a senior position. Tell them you can't join now.'

'It doesn't work that way.'

Scenario two: You are at your wit's end trying to find a maid.

'Why don't you ask your mother-in-law to send you one?'
 'I checked. It seems people from Delhi don't want to come to Bombay. They don't like the weather. Or the flats.'
 'Just get someone from the village and train her.'
 'Yes, but I don't know anyone in a village. Do you?'
 'And you must get one for the house and one for the baby. Oh, and a third as a back-up in case any of these two quits.'
 'Yes, and where do I live?'

Scenario 3: You are complaining that the baby keeps you awake and you are sleep deprived.

'Isn't he six months? Start weaning him now. Else you will have trouble later.'
 Or
 'You must read those books where they teach you how to put the baby on a schedule. My daughter-in-law is doing a great job of it.'

Grandmothers of course have their own agenda on what to do with the newborn, and somehow, handing him to a maalishwali seems to top the list. Dialogues with the mother become increasingly unbearable at this point.
 'When should I call the maalishwali? The baby is already a week old.'
 'No maalishwali is going to touch my baby. Even the paediatrician said so.'
 'These modern doctors don't know anything. How do you think you and your siblings grew up?'

'He is too small for all that. Anyway all this maalish business is rubbish.'

'Do what you want then. I am only telling for your own good. You will see how nice and strong his bones will become with maalish. Even his butt needs shaping.'

'There is nothing wrong with his butt!'

I later heard her hushed whining on the phone to a certain aunt on how I was 'so adamant' and wouldn't listen to anything she had to say.

My camera was a pleasant distraction for me in the initial months, as I went on about mundane chores of changing nappies, burping, feeding, walking and rocking the baby every two hours. Taking pictures, documenting my baby's growth through my Facebook albums kept my sanity alive.

I was rudely awoken one day.

'Don't take pictures when the baby is sleeping. It's not good for the baby.'

'Please put a black teeka before you take pictures.'

'Don't post pictures on Facebook. You never know who's looking at them.'

The advice never stops. Once I happened to tell an aunt that the baby was passing gas. She was quick with a remedy.

'Crush some garlic, saute in some cooking oil, add a pinch of asafoetida, and rub this oil on the baby's belly button.'

'Really?'

'Yes, the farts will disappear.'

But can the garlic and hing (asafoetida) travel through the belly button?

'Trust me. I have also brought up four grandchildren.'

I don't know about the baby, but I had a tough time surviving the smell of garlic and asafoetida overnight, and realised a few farts wouldn't hurt. And that was the end of it.

Baby Byte:
Please stop this hing nonsense. I might develop body odour.

Then there is the whole sermon on co-sleeping (which I chose for my child). Somehow everyone has an opinion on it, and more often than not, the subtext is your (non-existent) sex life.

'Don't make the mistake of the family bed.'
'He will grow up to be emotionally manipulative.'
'He will never leave your bed, mind you!'
'You will just make him more clingy.'
'He has to learn to fall asleep by himself.'

There will be more advice and tips. How to increase your milk supply. How to make sure the baby sleeps in the night. How to improve the stools of the baby. How to reduce colic. How to bathe the baby. How to swaddle. How to massage. How to sleep when baby sleeps. How to get your strength back. How to make your stomach disappear. How to get your libido back.

One aunt sent me a strange packet containing dubious looking roots and barks a few weeks after I had given birth.

'Please rub these on a stone and allow the child to lick the extract from your fingers.'

'For what?'
'Your milk is not enough.'
'How do you know? You haven't even met me.'
'I am telling you, it isn't.'
'How will these roots and barks help?'
'They have nutrients. Iron. Many things.'

My mother actually believed her and was going to give my

child a lick of this concoction when I threatened her with dire consequences.

Another aunt called one morning to ask if I was 'making' enough. I knew what she was referring to.

'Yes, I think so. He seems satisfied.'

'Are you eating methi ka laddoos in ghee?'

'I hate those.'

'You must eat at least two a day. My daughter had them, and she was overflowing with milk.'

'But I feel like throwing up when I eat them!'

'Just do it for the baby.'

'But I am having enough fluids, juices, salads, soups.'

'All that raw stuff is rubbish. Juices just dilute your milk. These modern doctors don't know anything.'

But people don't stop at advice for the present and how to deal with it. They will also ask you the inevitable 'Are you planning another one?'

We were in Goa with the boy, shortly after his first birthday, lounging on hammocks, enjoying the sea, sun and sand when the owner of the resort got chatty.

'Don't take this the wrong way, but try and have the second one as soon as possible. It's better to finish it all off in one go.'

'Finish?'

'My son is two years and my daughter is two months. We planned well. Now we are set.'

He was thrilled he had managed his family logistics so well.

My yoga buddy Shraddha said, 'Don't waste time. Just have the second one quickly. Within a few years, you will be done with both, and they will look after each other.'

Is one ever done?

Baby Byte:
If you want to have the second one, it is your choice. Don't make it about me. I never said anything.

8
The Birth Mutiny

When I was a little girl, one night, my cat climbed into my bed and burrowed herself in the space between my ankles. At around 4 a.m., I felt something wet around my feet. I woke up to see that she had given birth to four kittens and was licking them clean off her placenta. The next morning, she was out, hunting for garden lizards, leaving her babies in my care.

There are few women in this world, perhaps the tribal women as we call them, who give birth in this way – noiselessly, without much fuss, drama or intervention. They are the only ones who return to their regular routines or bodies faster than any of us after giving birth.

The human race is ironically the only one where babies don't decide how they are born. Strangely, neither do mothers, although there is a lot of information available for them to be empowered with. If that isn't enough, there are birth support groups, blogs, doulas, prenatal consultants and birth educators. But despite knowing it all, and having a definite birth plan, most mothers still succumb to procedures considered routine by hospitals, doctors, and the caregivers.

A typical pro-natural birth plan would insist on the mother being allowed to drink and eat during labour, to keep the number of vaginal examinations minimal, to deliver in a normal room and not be taken to the operation room, to have no episiotomy (cut in the vaginal area) unless absolutely necessary, to have her husband and midwife be with her during labour, to have the baby placed on her chest immediately after birth even before cutting the cord, to cut the cord only after it has stopped pulsating. Basically, to let things happen naturally and have the doctor around to support in case of emergency and not interfere with unnecessarily.

Having a partner and ob-gyn who can see your point of view and make a birth plan with makes things far easier. Because when you are that heavy, you are in no position to defend yourself, and hence need a good lawyer. Most women feel shocked and violated at the rapid turn of events during birth and agonise over their birth stories for months after. My only advice to pregnant women is to take their time choosing their ob-gyn. This is perhaps the most important decision during pregnancy, almost as important as choosing the man to make the baby with. There is no rushing into this decision. Just like you don't have to marry the first guy you date, you don't have to go with the first doctor you consult with. Having chosen one, and expressing all your concerns to him/her, you might, at some point have to step back and be convinced that he/she will only act in your interest.

Perhaps the biggest myth to be busted in the whole childbirth process is that of the 'normal' birth. Technically, a normal delivery is a non-interventionist, natural, vaginal birth. How many of these have you heard of?

When people say 'normal' what they are implying is natural birth, which is so not the case, ninety-nine percent of the time. 'Natural' birth, as the word suggests, is how nature intended it. Which means your body tells you when it's ready to give birth, and you do a series of things that make it comfortable for you to do it. Like squat, or take a sip of water or pace around restlessly, looking for a comfortable spot (like my cat did), and well, just do it! It is not a medicalised birth by any means. Sometimes, you might be helped by a midwife or a doula, but only in as much as making it smoother for you, and in no way terrorising you to push or breathe or whatever it is they normally tell you to do. Haven't we all heard of women in the villages who disappear into the wilderness when they go into labour and squat to give birth? Well, that's natural birth.

But even so, every woman thinks she is going to have a perfectly normal delivery especially if her pregnancy has been more or less stress-free. (C-sections are things that happen to someone else.) 'Normal birth' as it is commonly referred to, is an anomaly in itself. Normal is not being made to lie on a bed and put on a gown. Normal is not having a retinue of doctors and nurses shouting 'Push, push!' at you. Normal is not being refused water or candy when you want it.

But, in reality (and some of this might gross you out, but is good to know):

- Asking a woman to lie in a supine position when her body is almost defying gravity (a prerequisite for a natural birth) is considered normal.
- Withdrawing any form of food or drink from the woman about to give birth is considered normal. (Although the body's natural response in times of stress is to chew or drink something.)
- Asking a woman to 'push' when her body tells her otherwise is considered normal.
- Giving her a synthetic oxytocin drip hours before her body is ready for labour, is considered normal. Although oxytocin (the hormone that induces contractions) is released by the body in adequate amounts at the onset of labour.
- Giving the woman an enema (which helps accelerate one of the routine bodily functions of egestion) is considered normal.
- Restricting the woman from any form of movement while all she is dying for is to pace up and down, is considered normal.

- Giving the woman a spinal anaesthetic or epidural, which immobilises her from waist downwards, and then asking her to push when she cannot feel a thing, is considered normal.
- Performing an episiotomy, which is a cut in the perineum (area between the vagina and the anus) for easy passage of the baby from the vagina, is considered normal. This, when the perineum is fully capable of tearing itself in adequate measure and healing the tear on its own.
- Shoving a suppository up the woman's rear or dousing her with a laxative for weeks after birth to ease passage of stools is considered normal.
- Taking the baby away to be bathed and put under UV light immediately after birth while all it needs is skin-to-skin contact with the mother is considered normal.

My friend Shaila recently gave birth to a baby girl. Around two days before her due date, her water broke. She was taken to the hospital where they started timing her contractions. Since the progress was not as prescribed, she was given oral prostaglandins (those hormone-like thingees that are supposed to make labour smooth). Four hours later, she was still not officially in labour, so she was put on a Pitocin drip (a synthetic hormone to induce labour). Six hours later, the contractions were still not that far apart, so more prostaglandins and another drip followed. By the end of the next evening, she could bear the pain no more and asked for an epidural. She still didn't go into labour and the epidural wore off in a few hours, so she was given the second epidural.

Finally, the doctors packed up at midnight saying the baby would probably be born the next morning. In two hours, she went into labour and was given the third epidural. By this point, she was too fatigued to push. So two of the doctors applied fundal pressure (where they actually press your abdomen from the outside, trying to force the baby into the birth canal), performed an episiotomy, and the baby was finally yanked out with forceps. Needless to add that she (the baby) was shocked, traumatised and refused to cry. She had also contracted an infection on account of the mother being in 'dry' labour for thirty hours, and was sent to be kept under observation.

It was a 'normal' delivery.

(Incidentally, under 'normal' fall 'induced', 'forceps' and 'suction' births.)

Her ob-gyn later told her that if her baby was even hundred grams heavier, they would have had to perform a C-section. This was supposed to make her feel better.

She was discharged a week later.

Baby Byte:
Don't rush us because your patience is running out. We like to take our time and we hate being yanked out!

That C-section Mafia

When you are pregnant, you are always warned about the dreaded C-word, about doctors in the fast lane who plan their vacations around your due date, and hospitals who have set their C-section fangs on you and will exploit you when the time comes. You are to be on your guard with such doctors, you are told by birth networks, friends, mommy predecessors and so-called childbirth educators.

In routine birth discussions, including a pro-natural birth networking group that I was part of, normal and caesarean births are talked about as the haves and the have-nots. Those of us that had C-sections are made to feel short-changed for the rest of our lives because we didn't have a 'normal' delivery Even those manicured baby books that show cosy pictures of serene women surrounded by picture-perfect bassinets apologetically allot one hurried paragraph in the end to the C-section victims.

C-sections are looked at as failures. People who are plain lazy. Or shit scared. Like the guy who could not pass in his exams, but got grace marks and was pushed to the next grade. When you have a C-section, you will have enough of 'Poor you! You had a C-section!' What they are thinking, but not saying is: 'So you took the easy way out? Didn't have the balls to push, eh?'

So you go along building this 'good vs evil' image in your head about normal and C-section births. And then you also hear about the more exotic, yet natural birth options, like hypno-birthing, water birthing, or even home birthing with the support of a doula. You wish you could opt for those if only you had the support of your partner/family right till the very end. They of course, dismiss it like it is some childish whim of yours.

Don't get me wrong. I am not advocating C-sections or pooh-poohing normal deliveries. What I have a problem with is either of them being orchestrated to make babies arrive before they are ready.

Baby Byte:
I don't care if 9 is a lucky number. If I want to be born on the 13th, it is my problem.

I thought I was a great contender for a normal birth. I had a breeze of a pregnancy, did Iyengar yoga, went to work till my ninth month, had no complications, ate well, never threw up, had excellent test reports, and was very active and in great health and spirits.

Around week thirty-seven, I felt some turbulence within. It was like an earthquake just happened. At first I thought the baby had engaged (positioned itself in the pelvic cavity just before the onset of labour). But that was supposed to make you feel lighter on the ribs. I felt heavier instead. I called my ob-gyn who told me to do a sonography.

The results showed that my baby had turned breech. He was now head upwards, leg downwards, and looking down at the world from a vantage point where he seemed very comfortable now. I was later told it happened to all small women as their pelvis lacks room for the baby's head to engage.

I furiously read up on the Internet and found that there was a slim chance of breech babies turning back again. I got heaps of advice.

'Try visualisation. Draw the image in your head. Imagine your baby doing a gentle somersault inside, and it will happen.'

I pretended to direct my own little movie of my breech baby straightening out, but no luck.

'Try hoisting your pelvis high up in the air and lying down with a pillow under your shoulders. You will create space in your pelvis, and the baby will be drawn to it,' said a yoga expert.

Turns out, the baby was enjoying looking up at my pelvis.

'Do somersaults while swimming.'

This I found ridiculous and impractical, considering how bottom heavy I felt and somersaulting suddenly didn't feel like one of my skills.

'Talk to the baby, ask it to turn again.'

I would sit up in bed in the middle of the night, asking Tia (my name for the baby girl who eventually turned out to be a boy) to turn back, so that her extremely fit mommy could have a natural, vaginal birth. Nothing.

'Write letters to the baby.'

'Try Reiki. Prayer. Magnetotherapy.'

'Have you tried Homeopathy? There is this wonder pill called Pulsatilla 200.'

'Flower remedies. Hypnotherapy.'

I tried some of the above and gave up, feeling a bit silly and desperate. I still read up all I could on ECV (External Cephalic Version), in which the ob-gyn turns the baby manually, inch by inch, by pushing it from the outside. He tried, and the baby almost made it, but decided it was happier in the breech position, causing major turbulence once again! Like my ob-gyn said, 'Maybe it is just more comfortable this way. Let's not fight nature too much.'

I decided to enjoy my defiant baby finally. The words C-S-E-C-T-I-O-N were looming large, as I was told no private hospital would risk a natural birth for a breech baby (apparently, the risk was far higher than for C-sections).

I was despondent. My ob-gyn then told me something I still remember: 'There is a reason the baby has turned. Let's not do too much to undo it. Yes, you might have a C-section, but you might as well go into it with the right frame of mind. If you think you are going to be miserable after a C-section, you probably will.'

I decided to stop worrying and just trust my ob-gyn completely, and believe that he would only do what was best for me. That day on, something changed. I embraced my impending C-section and stopped fighting it. It worked. It certainly made me calmer. Yes, I did feel the tug of my stitches for a few weeks and although I was walking around the next day, it took me a while to be truly mobile, drive my car, go to the market, the parlour, the movies. Perhaps eight to ten weeks. But I look at it this way – at least I didn't go through twenty odd hours of invasive labour, a bad episiotomy and the resulting constipation. You win some, you lose some.

Even so, the minute you announce you've had a baby, you will be asked, 'Normal or caesarean?' It almost appears like they are filing it away as some useful piece of information.

But what is worse is the post-mortem. When I told a fellow mommy I just met at a La Leche League (a breastfeeding support group) meeting that I had a C, she sighed and said, 'Oh, no!' I reminded her that my baby turned breech and a normal vaginal delivery could not be possible. Her reaction: 'Are you sure it was breech?'

If I was feeling a bit low about my longer recovery period, this set me back further.

Parul, a friend of mine who bounced around through most of her pregnancy and was slated to deliver in Australia (where her parents live) got the shock of her life when, in her eighth month she was told that she couldn't fly. That the baby's blood pressure had dropped and it would be detrimental to put any further stress on him. A few days later, she was told she had to go in for induced labour and should check into the nearest hospital. Since there was still a month for her due date, she was shattered. This is not what she had bargained for. Anyway, after a traumatic C-section which made her feel completely violated, the baby was born, one month too soon.

'I wish I had read up about C-section,' she said to me later. 'I just kept reading more and more about natural birth as I thought I would definitely have one. I felt so cheated.'

She didn't recuperate well and went into hibernation post-baby and only surfaced after a year, still resentful and broken. She put the fear of the C in me and told me to fight it, whatever happened.

Another friend, Mythili, opted for hypno-birthing, but had a bad time with an episiotomy gone wrong at the end. Apparently, she was cut too deep and bled so much that her haemoglobin dropped to six and she had to be given iron injections to recuperate. When I asked her why she didn't put her foot down for the episiotomy, she said she was too fatigued to fight. To add to her misery, her baby just wouldn't latch on to her breast, and she was dying of the pain of engorgement.

When I heard these stories, my C-section story didn't seem that bad. I went full-term, my water broke, so I knew my baby had given a sign (I didn't want to choose a date and go elective). My ob-gyn did try a last minute external version (turning back of the baby to the head down position), the epidural did take effect almost immediately, the surgery did wrap up in ten minutes, the baby (all 3.3 kgs of him) was put to breast immediately after the cord stopped pulsating and was cut off, the latching on was immediate and smooth, the milk machine did work as planned and breastfeeding was a success from the word go. Plus, he was gorgeous and had my cleft and curly hair. I was ecstatic, although my stitches hurt every time I laughed. Or sneezed.

I was discharged on day four and no one believed me when I told them I had a C; they expected me to be lying like a wounded soldier. I was up and about, although in discomfort, but my face belied my real feelings. I was doing yoga by month three and returned to my pre-pregnancy size by month five. I was lauded by one and all. Only I knew that my body had been permanently altered. The scar on my bikini line and my pelvic wattle (the overhang) will stay with me for life.

A quick word on the epidural, vouched for as God's gift to womankind. An epidural is like a bad relationship. Even after the boyfriend is gone, the tug still remains. And a part of you is altered forever. Before the anaesthetist gave me the epidural, he poked my arm in two different ways and explained to me the difference between pain and sensation. So what the epidural was going to do for me was to convert the pain into a mere sensation as my baby was being dug out. I thought that was liberating. I was wrong. I still feel the tug of the epidural, but life goes on.

Post C-section, there are women, like my friend Shagorika, who display a peculiar kind of bravado. 'It's nothing! I was up and about the next day. I decided to go elective for the second baby, since the first was an emergency C-Section.'

Women who say they don't feel a thing, are perhaps right in their own way. Perhaps they are not tuned enough to their bodies to feel its subtleties. Perhaps someone like me is deeply sensitive about small changes in my body, and couldn't help noticing that my backward bend in yoga now took more of an effort.

No, I am not a pain junkie. But the feminist uproar still amuses me. 'Why should it be our lot to suffer pain during childbirth?' is an argument that has made the epidural some sort of an emancipating device. It is far from that. If it gets in the way of doing things that matter to you later, of course it is not liberating. It trades a temporary sharp pain for a permanent dull one.

Baby Byte:
Why are you looking at me with those 'poor you' eyes? I am doing okay. It is mommy who might take a little longer.

Giving birth is like getting your first menstrual period. No one talks about it. You never share that story until you are prodded. Did things go as you thought they would? As you had planned? Was there a medical emergency? Were you told your baby's life was in danger? Did things seem too rushed for your liking? Did

you sense urgency or impatience in the medical staff around you when you were not 'performing' as you were told?

That is sure to open up a Pandora's box.

If the questions are never asked, a mother's real birth story never gets told.

Every woman is part of a larger birth chain – there are several births that she is party to, before she actually gives birth. First, your mothers had you. Then, perhaps you were around when a few of your aunts gave birth. Soon it was time for your friends to have theirs. No one has ever told you anything about birthing since you never asked. In a sense, all women are carrying some baggage about their birth stories – some told, some partly told, some never told. With a few exceptions, all stories have one thing in common: a feeling of shock and bewilderment – 'I didn't know this'; or a sense of betrayal – 'Why didn't anyone tell me this?' Like sex, birth stories also seem to be a taboo topic, with women preferring to lounge in the exotica of baby and new-found motherhood and selectively obliterate any form of painful or discomforting memories about childbirth and the embarrassment of their post-birth bodies.

Baby Byte:
Next time you have a baby, talk to people who will tell you the truth. Or read this book.

If only people told you or documented their birth stories exactly as they happened. But then I guess, the euphoria of motherhood veils everything. Behind the ecstasy, the agony gets hidden, smothered, almost nullified.

Perhaps it is some form of conquest. Women don't want to be seen as types who moan about their pregnancy or share their post-birth angst. And the faster they emerge looking as good as new, the more they are lauded. 'Wow, she was up and about in three weeks!' Perhaps it is competitiveness. 'If she can, I can.' Or maybe it's an attempt at reclaiming their lives. 'It's just a phase, it will pass.'

Now here is the tricky part. The baby does momentarily distract you from what you have gone through. It almost feels like yes, it was worth the unnecessary intervention. But that's just transient. Don't ever believe anyone who says, 'When you hold the baby, you will forget everything.' Because every woman remembers everything about her pregnancy and delivery (although there are flashes of amnesia), and recounts it whenever she is sharing with another woman who had gone through the same, perhaps, worse. Your birth story can very often, scar you for life. Talking about it, sharing it, even documenting it can help you come to terms with it. Sometimes this can take months, sometimes years.

Baby Byte:
The more you whine, the worse it is for us.

9
All About My Mother

'Amma, how was I born?'

The first time I asked my mother about her birth story (of me) was when I was pregnant. She had forgotten all about my birth. Upon probing further, here is what I got.

'I don't remember much. There wasn't any labour pain. The doctor checked me before leaving the hospital that night and said there was still time. An hour later, my contractions started. There were no mobile phones then. The nurse in charge noticed that the surname column in my file was blank, and asked me what it was. I said we didn't have surnames. She was taken aback. I told her, if she insisted, it was Iyer. She panicked, and I didn't know why. I later found out that a Mrs Iyer, who was a family friend of the ob-gyn, was also due to give birth. Word was sent to the doctor's house that Mrs Iyer was in labour, and he dashed back. It turned out to be the wrong Mrs Iyer, and you were yanked out by forceps. The Iyer name stuck!'

And that's how poor me was rushed into this world and happened to have a different surname from my siblings. Not exactly divine intervention, but there!

'Did I latch on? Did you have trouble feeding me? What about postpartum depression?' I wanted more.

My mother doesn't remember a thing except that she went to work when I was twenty-eight days old, leaving me with her mother.

Funny how pregnancy and motherhood fit into short-term memories in the minds of most women, our mothers included. We, of course, live in an era where labour and birth is so detailed and documented, that people remember at what week the baby kicked, and what week it engaged and what week you felt the first movement and all of that. Even sonograms make an appearance in baby albums. But things were much simpler when you were born; at least your mother made them out to be.

Pregnancy is somewhat of an equaliser between your mother and you. Remember the times when you two had serious differences and there was much drama, tears and emotional blackmail, and she would say, 'You will only understand this when you become a mother.'

'Don't give me that dialogue. I will never have a baby.'

'Never say never!'

In fact your pregnancy sends her into a flashback of her own pregnancy. It is a reminder for both of you – that you were in her womb, and here you are now, all grown up and ready to give birth to another one of you.

Through their daughters being pregnant, giving birth and all that, mothers get to relive a lot of their vulnerability. This is their chance to re-nurture a relationship that might have become too adult and grown up for its own good. In a strange way, your mother treats your womb like it was hers. It is a special time for her, a time not all mothers get to experience in their lifetime. Naturally, her protective instincts towards you will kick in all at once.

'Don't cross your legs. The child may get knotted in the umbilical cord.'

'How do you know?'

'I know, I have given birth too. Not once, but twice.'

But at some point, her over-protectiveness begins to get to you. Mothers thrive on the fact that they are mothers and you are the daughters. It is like a thing they have that you don't. Now that you will be a mother, too, you will find the mother playing her mother card much more.

Post baby, the grandmother equity sets in, and there's no way you can beat that.

'I don't think you should allow the cats in the baby's room. What if they harm him?'

'Amma, that's nonsense. I want my child to grow up with animals.'

'And I want my grandson to be protected by them.'

It's hard to argue that. But slowly, with supervision, I made her realise that they meant no harm, and in fact, provided a lovely sibling bonding in the absence of real siblings.

The more advanced you are in your pregnancy, the more connected you feel to your mother. Most women really want their mothers around or during childbirth, and definitely during the first few months after giving birth. Of course you and your mother are as different as chalk and cheese – the way you cook and eat, your approach to baby care, your parenting philosophies. But there are still things only she can do for you, things that you can only ask her to do for you, temper tantrums that you can only throw at her. It's tough to pop your boobs out with such abandon every hour in front of anybody else, even your husband. And no one else can understand your postpartum mood swings like your mother can.

Baby Byte:
I love grandmothers. Especially the ones who pamper my mommy, so she can pamper me!

Of course there will be the minor hiccups. There will always be 'her way' and 'your way.' She was a believer in maalish. I wasn't. She wanted the baby swaddled. I didn't. She wanted to powder the baby. I didn't.

Then there was the matter of ghee. And lactation. And nutrition. And rest.

'Here. Have this.'

'What is it?'

'It's a laddoo filled with good things. Dry fruits. Nuts. Methi. Ghee.'

'Amma, I don't feel like it. I hate the smell of ghee.'

'It's good for strength. You look weak.'

'What's wrong with me? I feel okay!'

'Just have it now that I have specially made it for you.'

'Whatever.'

Once she told me we should start feeding the baby formula in the nights so that I could sleep. I know now that she was thinking of me, but at that point, I went ballistic. The pro-breastfeeding purist in me was enraged.

'No way will my baby have formula.'

'Everyone gives formula. What's wrong with it? And they say mother's milk is never enough.'

'Who's they?'

I could never imagine being so vociferous with my mother-in-law. Plus I had gory visions of postpartum rage and depression and not wanting to be seen in that state by anyone other than my mother.

Some of my friends were not so lucky in the mother department and I realise how hard they must have had it. Naina's mother had passed away by the time she had her baby, Preeti's was too hands-off, Minu's was in fragile health and could hardly hold the baby. I considered myself blessed and I can never forget how much my mother helped me during the hardest time of my life, and how much I took her for granted.

I did not realise it then, but I do now – that while I looked after my baby, my mother looked after me. She made sure I ate well, and on time, that I rested, that I didn't have to stress about mundane stuff like vegetables and fruits, groceries and menus and maids. She made *rasam* on demand, bathed my baby, changed him umpteen times, went out in the pouring rain to get my adaptor repaired when my breast pump stopped working, had tea and breakfast waiting for me when I woke up, looked after my baby when I went back to work. She did all this without ever putting pressure on me to find a baby-maid, which was a huge challenge in itself. She obviously put her life on hold for me, for as long as I needed her. I owe her a great deal for making my baby and me her priority number one.

Motherhood is also an opportunity to renew your relationship with your mother-in-law. If you've had a great relationship, the baby will just help cement it. If you haven't, well here is your chance to have one. After all, she has the potential to be a caregiver, for whatever length of time, so perhaps it is her chance to give back as well.

My friend Geetu was full of gratitude for her mother-in-law. 'She was there for me when I needed her the most. She did for me what my own mother couldn't do, since she didn't keep well.' Her mother-in-law was happy to babysit when required, and this helped Geetu resume work, join the gym, socialise. 'She made sure I was well-fed, she had my glass of warm milk ready for me in the night.' She oozed gratitude. I was jealous.

'Yes, we did have our differences in bringing up the child, but the fact that she was there for me, when I needed someone around so bad, cemented our bond even further,' said Geetu.

On the other hand, Aliya had both sets of parents visiting her after the baby arrived, turning her into a nervous wreck with their parallel, often contradictory opinions on just about everything from breastfeeding to co-sleeping to the baby-maid to sterilisation to baby number two. Needless to say, she sunk into a full-frontal postpartum depression.

I have several friends who couldn't put their foot down about long-stay visitors, a common post-baby syndrome. New moms have been inundated with in-laws, parents and a big fat entourage landing up and crashing at their house around the same time as the baby, making it look like a baby picnic. I know this is harsh, but anyone who is high maintenance and needs looking after more than you or the baby needs to go. Learning to say 'no' is the hardest thing about pregnancy and motherhood. The easiest person to say it to is your mother.

Baby Byte:
I don't care who you are, as long as you hold me and burp me well and give my mommy a break sometimes.

10

Much Ado About the Boob

Just as the hedonism of singledom was measured by serial dating and your ability to play the field, the benchmark of motherhood seems to be: How much milk can your breasts produce?

By the time you are barely done gloating over your newly acquired we-don't-need-no-underwire boobs, there is a whole big lactation war out there waiting to be fought and won. It is an area where advice will come gushing even if sometimes, the milk won't.

Lactation (the act of producing breast milk) is something that tilts the balance. There are women who have difficult pregnancies, long painful labours, severe medical interventions, but breeze through lactation. There are those who have a breeze of a pregnancy and childbirth, but are hit by a truck when they realise the baby is not 'latching on' or the milk hasn't shown up.

If women were obsessed with their wombs pre-pregnancy, it's the turn of the breasts in the postnatal period. Lactation is like the last feather in the cap of the pregnant woman. Nursing a baby soon after birth is a conquest, a victory, a pinnacle no less. Remember images from old Hindi movies where the woman heaves an almost orgasmic sigh when the little one latches on? We never knew then what 'emptying' the breasts meant. Formula for a new mother is still a four-letter word and signifies defeat, even though we have all been brought up as Farex babies, our mothers now tell us. The age of the boob is back!

Technically, 'latching on' is when the baby takes a good look at your breast and as if to say 'approved', positions its mouth correctly onto it and starts suckling effortlessly, and hopefully, doesn't choke. Eureka!

Baby Byte:
It takes some practice, but then you can breastfeed with your eyes shut. And it is the easiest way to shut us up.

If you are lucky (like I was), this can happen immediately after the baby is born. Sometimes, the latching on can take days, weeks, months to set right, and not all mothers have the will to wait it out. When a baby doesn't latch on, it almost feels like you are being dumped. Or as though the baby is putting you through further tests till it is satisfied that your lactation machine is baby-certified.

Although it is always made out to be some sort of manufacturing defect in the new mother, there can be many reasons for a baby not latching on – mother-baby separation post birth, extra intravenous fluids during surgery or birth, over drugging or trauma during birth, engorged breasts or general anaesthesia. To add insult to injury, there are the self-appointed breast doctors in the guise of family who are busy pronouncing verdicts on your 'flow' or your 'supply' and whether it is 'good enough'. No wonder milk, rather the lack of it, is one of the major causes of postnatal depression. I later learnt that there is no such thing as 'not enough milk'.

Shikha, a friend from yoga class, had trouble with latching on, and she now tells me it was further compounded by the dozens of relatives who were visiting from her husband's ancestral town to see the first male child of the generation. 'Is the milk enough?' was the first question each one asked. Political correctness and privacy clearly belonged to another time and people. She was in pain, feeling dejected, engorged and now confused. She had all the milk and yet the baby wouldn't feed and was crying inconsolably. It took ten weeks for her baby to latch on, by the end of which she nearly had a nervous breakdown.

Vrushali, mother to a five-month-old, went through a lot of angst during breastfeeding. She said she felt excruciating pain each time she nursed and couldn't understand how it was made out to be the most natural thing for a new mother.

'The beatific breastfeeding mom is the next biggest lie after love. At least it took a huge toll on me because I was constantly in pain, constantly angry, constantly confused. I plodded on for five months not out of masochism, but because it was the best thing for my child. The day I could put a bottle to her mouth, I did.'

Another friend, Mona, had a very slow recovery from her C-section, and to add to it, she had a lump in her breast which made feeding excruciating. She also felt emotionally blackmailed into doing it by her family and resented that. Every time she gave up because she couldn't bear the pain, she was made to feel guilty. She said she kept trying, and one day, switched to the bottle.

Baby Byte:
I don't care if you had formula. I prefer the real stuff.

Perhaps her story would have had a happier ending if she had the right information, resources or support at the right time. Like a lactation consultant, or access to a La Leche League (an excellent and very committed support group for breastfeeding mothers). This group believes that anyone can breastfeed; some just require more support, guidance and perseverance than others. There is a very small percentage of women who genuinely have a problem in the milk-production department, but most of us can always make enough for our own babies. Some, of course, can feed a playgroup. If you are pregnant, now is the time to get the numbers of the La Leche League leaders in the city (they are also on Facebook and Google). You will be spending a lot of time talking to them after giving birth to your baby.

Lactation is big business. So are lactation laddoos, special barfis doused in ghee, and dairy-rich food to make you sick. I later found out that all you need is a wholesome diet, and perhaps just enough fluid to quench your thirst – whether it's juices, soups, water-rich fruit, or herbal teas. It's quite simple really. The more you feed, the more you make.

But, like many other women, I too was struck by the Methi Police.

It started with an aunt whose daughter had given birth just a few months earlier and she was the current custodian of all things lactation in the family.

'Ask her to have methi dosas and methi sabzi everyday. Also methi in her dal, soup, maybe salad too.' She told my mother. My mother told me. I barked.

'But I am producing enough for the baby, thank you!'

'What's the harm with more milk?'

My mother was clearly on a methi mission for the next few days. A suspicious bottle of fenugreek tablets made its appearance. Soon followed methi laddoos, methi parathas, methi dosas, methi kadhi, methi paneer and what have you.

And before I was fenugreeked out of my bones, a screech of caution from a friend arrived. 'Stop this methi bullshit, else your perspiration and breath will smell of methi and that's the end of your sex life!'

All methi went out of the window, even though the sex life was nowhere back in sight.

Baby Byte:
Please remember, we prefer the plain flavour any day.
So, easy on the condiments.

My friend Shagorika belonged to that six percent minority who had a genuine lactation problem which went undetected for three months. Her baby's weight gain was only fifty grams between the second and third month, which is way below the norm. She was asked to give eight formula feeds a day after breastfeeding. Manual pumps did not work on her and a good automatic one yielded thirty ml after forty-five minutes. Clearly, there was a milk drought. She felt cheated, angry, helpless, and did everything she was asked to improve her milk supply – Shatavari, Leptaden (herbal supplements that stimulate lactation) along with a diet rich in cumin seeds, dalia, ghee and other milk-producing agents. 'It was frustrating, because I was housebound, and I didn't know who to turn to for advice. The doctors were not of much help and my baby was suffering.'

The problem is, paediatricians are not experts in boobology, neither do ob-gyns think of boobs as their domain. So both are usually at a loss to help you with lactation issues. Some of them will recommend you to a lactation consultant; others might just be your alibis in formula-feeding. I was lucky to have a nursing staff post delivery that was totally pro-breastfeeding, and made it their collective mission. My doula, Lina, also hand-held (rather breast-held) me for the first few days and made it look less arduous than I thought, while my La Leche League leaders Yasmin and Kavita taught me how to read my baby. I always found nursing to be the easiest way to calm my baby.

Another friend, Sameera, had a more painful breastfeeding story. She grappled with several bouts of breast infection while nursing each of her daughters.

'What was terrible the first time I battled one (while breastfeeding my first daughter) was the total lack of information about it. No one seemed to be able to help me – neither the paediatrician and gynaecologist, nor older mothers around me. Most took it casually, making me out to be fussy, not realising the awful searing pain I was suffering. There would be nights on which I would feed my daughter with such terrible pain in my right breast that I would be crying. I tried to pump from that breast and feed her via bottle for one feed (so I could rest that breast), but she refused to take the bottle. But luckily over time, the pumping action of the manual breast pump helped release a nerve, and resolve the infection. I don't know what it was, but the pain subsided after two months. I have, however, been left with a permanent lump in my right breast which doctors spend a lot of time peering at when I go for a mammogram or breast ultrasound.'

The second time Sameera had that same pain with baby no. 2, she was better prepared – 'I had meanwhile read up a lot online and in books, and spoken to some others who suffered similarly, and identified it as a breast infection that had not been treated, as it should have been with a course of antibiotics. This time, it was diagnosed rightly and I took a seven-day antibiotic course (which was safe enough for me to continue breastfeeding), and felt better.' In the months that followed, she battled two more such infections.

Although she nursed both her daughters for twelve-thirteen months, Sameera believes it's a personal choice and that at no stage should the working mother be made to feel guilty about her choosing work over baby and breastfeeding, should she choose not to continue it. 'I see enough women berating themselves over this. Having doctors and other judgemental breastfeeding mothers doing so does not help.'

Once the lactation clock starts ticking, it's a race to finish first (or last, depending on which side of the weaning philosophy you are on). The World Health Organization (WHO) and most doctors recommend exclusive breastfeeding for the first six months. So most women plan their careers, their sex lives, the next baby, their tummy tucks, whatever, by factoring this in. Clocking in these six months means ticking off a major milestone in the whole motherhood business.

During this period, every conversation with a fellow nursing mother inadvertently turns into a lactation journal.

Woman A: How often do you feed?

Woman B: I think ten times a day. Maybe twelve?

Woman A: That's it? I end up feeding at least fifteen-sixteen times a day. I am just making too much milk I guess. My breasts are engorged all the time.

Woman B: Maybe you should express.

Woman A: I do! Sometimes I can fill four bottles at a time. I think I have enough milk to feed the city.

By this time, Woman B is feeling really small and dejected, wondering if she is milk-challenged and quickly calling experts to figure out how she can produce more.

Baby Byte:
Don't believe anyone who says your milk is not enough.
Ask me.

Almost everyone starts out a believer in breastfeeding. Passionate, committed, patient. But when feeds get longer and more frequent and me-time becomes more and more elusive, women begin to find their ways around it. Expressing milk is the one thing that can help you get your life back, at least one hour at a time...the hour that you can use to wax your legs or get that pedicure.

And then more advice will come your way. When I told Anu that Re always woke up during the nights for a feed after month five, she had a tip.

'Just disappear when it's time for the baby's last night-feed. Go and sleep in another room, read, watch TV, do whatever. Get the husband to feed it expressed milk. If the baby forms that association, he will know not to expect you for the rest of the night.'

'Really? It works?'

'Yes. For the baby, out of sight is out of mind, so if they don't see you, they just sleep through. As long as they get the milk.'

Sounded like a perfect plan, except I didn't realise how hard it could be to always stay 'one feed ahead' of the baby, especially when you are nursing all the time in the first few months, and there is no real window to express. And should you accidentally spill one expressed feed, you've had it. Total pandemonium and you are back to square one.

Minal had another express tip.

'When you wake up, express for a full half-hour before you feed the baby. This way, you can build your stock.'

'But the baby is up too, and wants to be nursed.'

'That's okay, it can have the expressed milk from your stock, and you can stay ahead.'

Logistically, it made sense, but I found it a bit odd to feed the baby from a bottle, while I was pumping away to make more bottles.

Privacy also is a much underestimated thing in the whole breastfeeding business. I was lucky to live in a two-bedroom apartment with just my mother and my baby around most of the day. For many women, this is not so. There are small flats, more people to deal with, and seldom does the mother have a room for herself and the baby where she will have no intruders. My friend Suman actually weaned her baby off prematurely as she felt awkward nursing in the presence of her in-laws who lived with her, and would walk into the bedroom abruptly to use the loo, without even knocking.

Baby Byte:
Please don't stop cold turkey. It is as painful for us as it is for you.

In my case, after the initial clumsiness and hiccups, breastfeeding had more or less been a breeze and the easy way out most of the times. I fully endorse it and would recommend it for as long as you can. Breast milk is full of good stuff, builds immunity for the baby and protects it from disease, besides offering emotional and physical security. Yes, it takes work, but in the end, it is totally worth it.

But one of the ironies of breastfeeding is that the buck will always stop with you. *Baby is crying = Baby needs milk* is a weapon used by husbands, family, friends, strangers, anyone, everyone. It is something that absolves anyone else from the care-giving process. 'Got milk? Give breast' seems to be the easy way out for anyone who doesn't want to hold a baby for longer than two minutes.

After having been to several La Leche League meetings, and exchanging stories about nursing and related hurdles and complications, I have come to realise the multi-layered aspects of nursing. And how much strength and perseverance it takes to keep it going, and how our society is strangely anti-lactation even though it claims to be otherwise. First of all, there are really no public spaces to nurse. Women are constantly being asked to wean, else the child will get exploitative, they are told. In such a scenario, to stick it out is no mean feat. Post the first few months, not a day passed when I didn't get asked, 'When are you planning to wean?'

Nursing became my little secret. Despite all the scary stories and the formula fiends around me, I chose to go the full-boob way. It was a no-brainer to me. The choice was natural vs processed. I chose natural, like I always do. It's a decision I have never regretted, despite the fact that there were days when it got overwhelming and I felt like I needed a breast sabbatical. Or there were days when I just missed my cleavage-enhancing underwire bras and hated the sight of my mommy bras. Or days when I wondered when I would ever have my breasts to myself. Or days when I was reminded of the song, 'Stuck in the middle with you' from Reservoir Dogs, whenever my little boy demanded his elixir, pointing to my girls, and exclaiming, 'Mimmi!'

But I had a smiling baby most of the time (he smiles more than most babies even now), and I hardly ever saw the doctor (yay for super immunity). More importantly, by giving him the emotional security through the constantly nurturing physical contact that comes with nursing, I was perhaps helping him become his own person. The bond it formed between us was just too special to tamper with. Maybe I am a lazy mom. I learnt to diffuse any situation, any tantrum, any crying fit, any irritability just by popping out the boob. It always worked. There were the minor hiccups of nursing in public in an emergency, but I learned to treat it as a wardrobe malfunction.

Baby Byte:
We like easy access and we don't want to be asked to work too hard for our food, negotiating tricky buttons or too much fabric.

But just when you make your peace with lactation and its vagaries, along come the lactation demons.

'Why don't you start formula?'

'Breast milk is never enough.'

'Babies are always hungry.'

'We have all given formula to our kids. Nothing wrong with it.'

They are the ones who will make nursing look like something of an ordeal. Something self-sacrificing and martyr-like. Something that need not be done. Something that should be substituted as soon as you can, so that you can move on to more productive, challenging things like career.

Sometimes, these are the feminists, fighting for the 'free the breast' campaign in the guise of gender issues of being chained down, ensnared by motherhood, or just keeping you from claiming your life back. Sometimes, it could be your own mother or your mother-in-law. My mother thought of me as gallant for continuing to nurse for such a long time. My mother-in-law told me that I could stop at six months, because that's when she had stopped feeding her son (my husband). She was shocked that I chose to nurse for three years. So is my friend Priya who has formula-fed her two boys right from the start. Incidentally, both of them suffer from huge eating disorders. When she asked me how I got my son to eat everything, I just pointed to my girls. 'I was generous with my boobs,' I said. Every time I see a child with eating and sleeping disorders, frequent visits to the doctor, one too many temper tantrums or unduly aggressive behaviour, I know why I chose to do what I did.

Mary J. Renfrew, a director from Mother and Infant Research Unit, UK states:

> There was also the first wave of feminism, which stamped into everyone's consciousness in the 60s, and encouraged

women to get away from their babies and start living their lives. So the one thing that might have helped – women supporting each other – actually created a situation where even the intellectual, engaged, consciously aware women who might have questioned this got lost for a while. As a consequence, we ended up with a widespread and declining confidence in breastfeeding, a declining understanding of its importance and a declining ability of health professionals to support it. And, of course, all this ran along the same timeline as the technological development of artificial milk and the free availability of formula. ... Giving up breastfeeding is not something that women do lightly. They don't just stop breastfeeding and walk away from it. Many of them fight very hard to continue it and they fight with no support. These women are fighting society – a society that is not just bottle-friendly, but is deeply breastfeeding-unfriendly.

I recently realised I was perhaps one of six women I knew in my city who believed in natural weaning and it raised many eyebrows. Sometimes, peer moms who didn't breastfeed got all defensive when they found out I was.

Peer Mom: How old is he now?
Me: Eight months.
Peer Mom: Eating solids?
Me: Yes.
Peer Mom: So is he on formula now?
Me: No, am still nursing him.
Peer Mom: What about cow's milk?
Me: No.
Peer Mom: Hmmm...but isn't it difficult, when you are out?
Me: No, I manage.

Lalita Iyer

Peer Mom: It was getting too stressful for me beyond five months. Besides she loves formula!

Keeping up with breastfeeding once you go back to work can be a tricky phase for a new mother. Paediatricians might often find themselves giving the nod to the bottle at this point. Perhaps it is what mothers want to hear. Most women don't think they can juggle their boobs, the job and the commute, so they just stop, cold turkey. This can be agonising for the boobs and the child. A bit of advance planning on the boob logistics and both mother and baby could be happier. Tapering feeds gradually, starting to express way before resuming work, talking to a La Leche League leader – all of these could help. Plus it is never an all or none. Even if a mother can manage a feed before and after working hours, it still counts as some elixir for a baby. It still means that much less stuff from a tin is going into his body.

Although I have done it, expressing at work is not as breezy as it's made out to be. When people say 'Why don't you express in your office?' chances are they haven't done it themselves. It's hard to find work places that have an attitude of empathy towards breastfeeding and also practical facilities (such as a place to pump milk and a fridge to store it) to aid it. I did my homework. I started discussions with my HR department even before I went on maternity leave. I told them I would need a private space to express milk, shelf space in the community fridge, and freedom to be excused whenever 'I had to pump'. It was an unusual and strange request, they informed me, but they were supportive. I found it hard to believe that because forty percent of the staff was women. Was I the first in the eighty-five-year-existence of the organisation who wanted to breastfeed post the three-month maternity leave period?

When I returned to work after three months, my breast-pumping cabin (to which I had the only key) was waiting. It was the only non-transparent cabin in the office, with huge posters appointed to mask it from ground to ceiling, and people generally speculating what was going to happen within, and me feeling happy about my little secret.

Off I went to work, armed with a hand-me-down double breast pump from my sister-in-law. Every few hours, or whenever my breasts beckoned, I would let myself into the cabin with my oversized bag which had my pumping ensemble, and not emerge for half-an-hour at the very least. I usually had a book to keep me company.

My expressing ensemble had nine crucial parts and one large bag to fit all of them which made me wobble a wee bit more than when I was pregnant. I am sure if someone really saw me assembling it all, they'd have thought I was a bomb-maker.

How a breast pump works:

There are two breast attachments or shields which are suctioned on or capped on to the breast (one or both, depending on your dexterity). One end of each is a receptacle for the milk. The other end is a tube connected to a suction pump which has a power source. The suction pump can be controlled at cycles or vacuum level, which can be adjusted. Oh, and I forgot, there are also two tiny valves which need to be clamped at the end of the nozzle where the receptacle begins.

This is for the apparatus. Now for the collectables. Each of the receptacles has to be emptied into storage containers (you need to have as many sets as the number of times you need to pump, because milk from 2 p.m. cannot be mixed with milk from 4 p.m.). Then you need a larger container, preferably an icebox, inside which all this can be kept. Plus lots of tissues/gauze/breast pads, a cup of tea, an adaptor to connect the various devices and voila! You are set.

Now even if one of these nine items is missing or ill-performing, the breast pump won't work. This has two side effects. One is, you will have to go home without any milk for your baby, which means your milk bank will be depleted, and you might reluctantly have to feed your baby formula. Two, and this is far more serious, unless you are able to manually express (which is painful), you will have to spend the entire day at work, with sore, engorged, painfully tender, oozing breasts, and you better have enough breast pads to soak them up. Not just that, you may also have to endure perhaps a two-hour meeting with a completely pointless agenda, where you are expected to make creative contributions to the discussion.

I still remember how horrified I was, when one day, soon after my induction into the breast pump, I actually forgot to carry the adaptor plug and realised I couldn't express. My boobs were already starting to hurt and there were still a good six hours to go before I could reach home. I called Kavita, my La Leche League goddess and she calmly told me to squeeze a little bit out by massaging my breasts, but not too much, else I would send a signal to my breasts to produce more milk, which wasn't required at that point. It felt a bit weird doing this in the loo, mopping up the spurts of milk in tissues. Would the ladies think I am some sort of sexual pervert? Anyway, I was beyond caring, because it had to be done and was the only way my breasts would stop hurting.

There could be various impediments to pumping at work, apart from excusing yourself every few hours to say you have some business to finish. Sometimes, when you are pumping, a colleague might call you on your cellphone and ask you where you are. Which is not the worst thing. What's worse is when the boss tells you, 'Can you come to my desk in two minutes?' And you are in the midst of harvesting your eight-ounce crop!

Once as I was pumping and on to my second bottle, which I was very proud of, someone started pounding on the door. Now the security had already been cautioned that I was not to be disturbed unless there was an emergency. I hollered from inside: 'Having a meeting here.'

'When will you be done?' Someone asked.

'About fifteen minutes.' I said, looking at my harvest, feeling sorry for my engorged second breast, still waiting to be liberated.

'Can you hurry up?'

Apparently the marketing team had to meet the agency for a presentation and there were no conference rooms available that day.

That was the beginning of the end. In about two months, I quit. Not the nursing, the job.

11

Up and About

Popping a baby alters your mind and body in significant ways. It's easier for the body to get on with the motions: breastfeed, burp baby, rock, clean poo, wash nappie, take a bath, bathe baby, breastfeed, clean poo again, change nappy, breastfeed, eat your lunch, breastfeed, burp, change nappy, oops take a loo break yourself, breastfeed again, burp, sing, make funny faces, clean poo again. This time check colour of poo because you forgot last time, and damn, have you written down how many wet and soiled nappies? So write it down. Wait a minute, where is that bloody diary you wrote in yesterday?

It's harder on the mind though. You do not automatically turn into mother mode the second after you give birth – there is angst, conflict, confusion, sometimes leading to depression – commonly referred to as PND (postnatal depression) or more commonly, PPD (postpartum depression). You will perhaps be shocked that none of those manicured baby books that taught you how to fold a nappy or what to pack in the hospital bag ever mentioned PND.

Here's why PND happens:

Birth trauma, too many interventions, loss of control: Maybe things didn't go as planned, and maybe your birth plan went out the window when the baby's heart rate dropped and the ob-gyn decided to induce labour. Or something equally random happened and you gave birth in a not-so-happy fast-forward way.

Exhaustion and sleep deprivation: Giving birth is hard work, and then getting into auto-pilot work mode after it, as primary caregiver and food source is even harder. And if you were thinking of catching up on sleep, now that the baby is out, forget about it. What were you thinking?

Anti-climax: Now that the baby is out, it's all about him. No one is concerned about you. It hurts being sidelined, and not getting any presents.

Anxiety about coping and desire to be perfect: Putting undue pressure on yourself to be the perfect mom doesn't work, because you always feel you could do better. Whatever you may have read, motherhood comes by instinct and it's best to let it stay that way. We all get there eventually, and this is no time to be competitive.

Postnatal disorders: All your body parts will protest against the upheaval of birthing, sometimes individually, sometimes in unison. So you may have back pain, wobbly fingers, tightness or itchiness around C-section stitches, mastitis, painful episiotomy stitches that make it difficult to sit, constipation, haemorrhoids, or a combination thereof.

No exchange, no refund: Having a baby is an irreversible process – there's no going back now, and suddenly motherhood may seem very overwhelming.

Baby Byte:
I know you are feeling low, but please don't take it out on me. And please don't talk to whiny moms.

Very often, the blues are from body image – not being able to claim one's body back soon after, figuring out that pregnancy fat doesn't disappear when the baby comes out. Plus, you always have to think of 'is-it-nursing-friendly?' whenever you choose to wear anything. Your hair is a mess and there's not much you can do about it, you need a wax real bad, but don't know when to get it, you probably smell of baby stuff when you go out, and even a movie date with a friend requires logistical planning of the highest kind. Many women also sense a loss of control over career, whether you choose to go back to work or stay at home. To top it, your libido has evaporated!

Some of us cope by talking to others, especially women who have been there before. Others might just withdraw into a shell and disappear for months, and you don't even realise they had sunk into depression. Most women carry their post-birth angst as a huge burden, never voicing it, or feeling it is inappropriate to.

Sometimes the postpartum blues continue for a few years after the baby is born, but in most cases they are an on and off thing. On days when you are feeling extremely low, and you happen to hang out with a group of women whose chief preoccupation in life is getting their nails and hair done, sipping Cosmopolitans, buying prêt-couture, tagging photos or updating their relationship status on Facebook – you wonder, where has your life gone? When did the baby become the single most important thing in it? Most importantly, where is the *you* in you?

Soon, the husband gets back to work and the visitors stop coming and then you are all on your own. This is when the calls stop coming, the initial baby pictures have been posted or emailed and the cooings and the gushings have stopped. Suddenly, the text messages reduce to a trickle and no one calls you except for mommies who perhaps birthed the same time as you. Friends who didn't show up at the hospital make their 'Call-if-you-need-anything' call. This actually means nothing. What you really need is friends who show up, spend a few hours with you, bring you food or cook a meal for you, are willing to watch the baby, walk it or rock it for a bit, or just do anything that makes your life a wee bit easier. Even if it is for an hour.

I'm Pregnant, Not Terminally Ill, You Idiot!

Most friends take the easy way out. 'I thought you might be busy, so I didn't call.' Or 'I didn't want to intrude.' Or act surprised. 'You texted back?' I felt like saying, this is my only link to the outside world, and besides, I can always manage one free hand. For a new mom, no friend can be intrusive, provided he or she is there, in person, with enough time and patience and you are not en route to something more exciting. 'I will just drop by for a bit' is not good enough.

Sometimes, all you need is a friend who was thoughtful enough to gift you a postpartum spa package. Or a massage. Or an hour of peace and quiet, with your feet up, and some music, while she watches the baby. Perhaps a pedicure? Or just time with you. Anything to take your mind off the postpartum discomfort or blues.

The thing about pain management is that it's like a one-night stand. Epidurals have short lives. It's like a lover who is not around for the rough road ahead. He's gone by the time you wake up.

Maybe no one told you this before, but here is what really happens after birth: First, *everything* hurts. And I mean everything. Your boobs, your abdomen, your pelvis, your calves, your back... well, what's left?

The good news is that your uterus is shrinking as we speak. Actually, as the baby suckles, your body releases prostaglandins which contracts the uterus. Only that you can feel the contractions; it's like a déjà vu of labour. Okay, period pain.

And they say, 'Oh, that always happens.'

Then there is a whole loosening of the fingers, to which they will say, 'Oh, that's nothing. It happened to me too.'

Mention it to the ob-gyn at the six-week visit and all he can do is remind you of postnatal exercises or 'Calcium, calcium, calcium!'

He will also overtly remind you that should you want to get pregnant again, you should work on it soon. At this point, you feel like hitting him.

And then you find it hard to pee and shit and you feel angrier. Then your breasts scream with the pain of engorgement every time you are out for a few hours, and they say, 'That's nothing!'

Baby Byte:
Please don't get engorged. It is as painful for us as it is for you. Have you ever tried drinking from a gushing pipe?

Then you get unmentionable things like constipation, which sometimes advances into piles or haemorrhoids, which make you scream in pain far greater than labour every time you want to 'go' and they say, 'Oh, these things are common in the first six to eight weeks after delivery.'

My friend Pooja summed up her post-birth angst quite nicely:

'The aftermath of giving birth is what no one really prepares you for. For years, women have been portrayed to make the entire child-bearing and rearing aspect look effortless. And that's the last thing it really is. It's plain hard! And I don't think there is any harm in admitting that. Women who admit that, are made out to be fussy. Just because it's been happening for centuries doesn't mean it's easy or not tough. I wish someone gave me a realistic view of what's to come. Beautiful ethereal images of women and babies that we have grown up seeing made me feel that something was wrong with me. I loved the experience, but it's not all perfect as it's made out to be.'

So why doesn't anyone tell you?

Why do they act like they are in a state of bliss? Why do they fake it so much?

Why do people pretend that the excruciating, debilitating

physical pain was never part of the programme and they have no clue how that could have happened to you?

The funny thing is, every time you mention a gory bit, all the gorier-than-thou stories emerge from the woodwork. These are stories that could be decades old, but were just saved up for a rainy day. Like a friend told me how she had to shove suppositories up her ass for two months post baby, because she *couldn't go*. Or another one who continued to look pregnant a year after the baby was born and was so embarrassed to step out, that she stayed indoors, nursing her depression.

I had a five-star birth, total comfort, candles in my room, music on my Ipod docking station, a great view of the sea, people I loved, a husband who loved me even more post my becoming a mother.

But there was still pain.

Your body feels like it has just been returned from the warehouse, fully wrenched and distorted, as though they opened something they could not put back together.

Most women have at least one demon – the epidural to remind them of childbirth. Some have several. I had a C-section even though I thought I was the perfect candidate for all things natural. But only you know that the bikini line scar just won't go away. Neither will the overhang which looks like a pelvic wattle. And every time I sat down or stood up in the initial months, I felt like a creaky cupboard.

Although it may seem as an imposition for some, the forty-day house arrest and ban from work after birth is actually a blessing in disguise. My mother told me not to do 'any work', just rest or sleep whenever I could. She meant it. For the time she stayed with me, all meals and beverages were just like room service.

Under 'work' also fell things like watching TV, reading the paper, checking emails, texting, or making a cup of tea. At that time, it irked me, but now I realise that household chores actually add up to a lot and rob you of the rest you have so earned. Reading, sitting in front of the computer – although they may seem routine – actually cause you to sit in one posture for long and strain your nerves. My aunt, a custodian of all things ritual would say, 'That's why we have the holier-than-thou forty-day house arrest. It is meant to provide as much rest to the mother as is physically possible. Else women would have foolishly got out and depleted their energies much sooner.'

The science to the whole thing is that it takes forty days for the uterus to shrink and generally for your body to recover from the major upheaval and hormone overload that it has gone through. The idea is to get as much rest as possible to recuperate and to not do anything other than baby-care.

Post baby, my friend Prachi came to visit, and me being my usual self, wanted to make her a cup of tea. She pinned me down to the sofa and said: 'Dude, your insides have just been put into a giant concrete mixer and churned and returned to you, so chill now. If you can get someone to get you a glass of water or make you a cup of tea, do it.'

How long you take to bounce back also depends on what kind of birthing experience you've had, and it is not as simple or normal as a C-sec. I thought having a normal delivery kind of insulates you from the postpartum woes, but what I saw around me was something else. Episiotomy seemed like the chief villain.

My friend Sandhya didn't realise she had an episiotomy until much later after the birth. Her stitches took two whole months to heal, as the cut was right up to her thigh and she was on super strong pain killers to keep her going.

'No one told me I had been cut that way. I now assume it was done because the baby's heart rate was dropping. It was the most painful experience I have had in my life. I did not sit properly for two months because of the way I had been cut or stitched.'

Nandini's was another case of an episiotomy gone wrong. She

wrote in to the pro-natural birth mommy network that I was a part of:

'I delivered a baby boy a month back; it was a Forceps-assisted delivery. Episiotomy was performed. Though it has been a month now, I am still in tremendous amount of pain, especially while walking and sitting. There is also a burning sensation alongwith itchiness near the tear area. Constipation is present, even though I have been taking laxatives. I have been taking painkillers and recently also took a course of antibiotics, but not of much help. The pain does not seem to reduce and it has been sometime already, getting worried about the recovery. What do I do?'

The stories unfold slowly, over a period of time. There are women you talk to everyday during your pregnancy, but you never hear their real stories until much later. It is as though you have to pass a very tough exam and demonstrate you are vulnerable in order for people, even your closest friends to share their stories.

When women exchange stories of birthing, they are actually wondering whether the other person was better off or worse off than them. If she was worse, it helps assuage her own pain. If the other one has a happier story, she is going to take that much longer to come to grips with her own. And yet motherhood is made out to be this ethereal, sublime experience which seems to obliterate every element of pain that featured in it. Perhaps pain is a short-term memory. Or maybe women are just in denial.

Women measure their birth victories by how soon they are able to get back into their old clothes or do what they used to do before they were pregnant (which could include smoking, drinking, clubbing till 4 a.m., or just going for a run on the beach, getting into their favourite bikini, whatever). They also measure it by how soon they can be 'seen' out there post birth.

Baby Byte:
The bikini can wait. Let me have some good food, please!

Technically, these benchmarks have been set by women for other women, which is a bit messed up, because we are trained to embrace the sisterhood and all that. But the longer a woman takes to come out 'in the open', the faster she gets labelled a loser. Some women never gain their original bodies back, and are often scoffed at in private, as if to say, 'Look, if this is what pregnancy does, I ain't going there.'

So what are the victory benchmarks post childbirth? Any woman will feel more jubilant if she shows no outward signs of having produced a child – protruding belly, dark circles, fat arms, sagging breasts. Or someone tells her, 'Gosh, you look just the same as before!' If she looks better than fellow singletons, great! If she can still score, even better! It might also help if she is not always physically saddled with the child, rather has a nanny-type person who does all of the manual stuff, and she, instead, poses for pretty mommy-baby pictures.

Baby Byte:
You waited nine months for me to be born and now you want your body back in three?

The whole pregnancy thing is a womb-upmanship of sorts, and it continues in the recovery from it as well. Every woman is measured by her ability to get 'up and about' in record time. If someone does it in three months, she has just raised the bar for others who can feel nothing but contempt for her. I used to feel a bit let down when statements like the following were made:

'She was up and about the next day.'

'It was easier for me to give birth than to have my eyebrows threaded.'

'I know someone who hit the gym in a week.'

I guess it begins at the beginning. One woman agonises over her morning sickness, 'Why do they call it morning sickness? I feel sick all the time!' Another will say, 'Oh, I never had any of that! My pregnancy was a real breeze.'

One will lament about her weight. 'My baby is fourteen months and I am still ten kilos overweight.' Another will slice her with, 'That's so weird. I went back to my pre-pregnancy weight in six weeks flat!' Supermodels will add further salt to your wound by saying they walked the ramp in six weeks. I have just two words of advice. Fuck them!

Everyone has a story. Some have been in labour for thirty hours, induced, and then C-sectioned. Some have labour as short as twenty minutes, but their placenta never came out and had to be surgically removed and they nearly bled to death and had to deal with abysmally low haemoglobin levels. Some had episiotomies that hurt for months, others had C-sections that healed in lesser time; some had babies that wouldn't latch on, or milk ducts that didn't open up, others were gushing like the rivers of Babylon but would rather the baby was on formula so they didn't have to feel tied down.

But, it's all one big secret. Every woman feels short-changed at some level by childbearing, but doesn't know whom to tell. She fears she might be the odd one out, and the secret stays with her until she has an opportunity to let loose. Or someone else shares

an equally gory story. Will talking about it make her look less cool? Less brave? Less maternal? Less resilient? Maybe it's a combination.

Baby Byte:
If you are sad, I'd rather you cry than fake laughter.

My friend Naseem had a fairytale of a pregnancy, never had any mood swings or discomfort, worked till the last day, went to the hospital, went into labour and gave birth in two hours. I secretly envied her.

When I met her a few months later, she told me how she had gone through one of the worst cases of postnatal depression ever. When her baby was twenty-one days old, there was a huge demand to 'see the grandchild' from both sides of the family, so she and her husband boarded a plane and landed in Delhi. That was the beginning of the end.

'Every day, there were various relatives who would drop in to my father's place unannounced, want to see the baby, hold him, spend time with him, not realising that I needed to spend some alone time nesting with my newborn. The house was huge, and I had trouble getting from one end to the other, and with a new born, everything adds up. I had no help whatsoever, and had I been in my space, my little apartment in Bombay, it would have been okay. But somehow, everything seemed like so much more work. The aunties were constantly instructing me and giving me advice on how to improve my milk supply. Every time the baby cried, they would pipe up "Maybe he is not getting enough". I tried to explain my angst and depression to my father, but he didn't get it.'

Since her mother was no more, she yearned for someone to fill into that role, which never happened. She would get weepy several times a day and just burst into tears. It was not enough for people to say 'call if you need anything'. 'I just needed someone to be there all the time. For me. Even if it meant getting me the baby's towel or a cup of tea. My husband, who I knew for eight years, tells me he had never seen this side of me.'

She returned to Bombay in two months thinking that at least it was her space and it would be okay. Within three weeks, she had in-laws visiting. 'It just became too much to deal with in a one-bedroom apartment. Every time I was nursing or changing the baby, someone had to use the loo. It was a small thing, but it made me hit rock bottom.'

It took Naseem six months to be rid of her postnatal depression. Perhaps her story put me on high alert, when I eventually gave birth six months later. So when the mother-in-law suggested that she visit me the week the baby was born, I asked her to, instead, come in a few weeks when I would really need her. It didn't go well. But at least I had one less thing to deal with.

Another friend, Chaitali, went to her mother's for her first baby. 'It was all good, the fuss, the pampering, despite too much "instruction giving" from older women in the family.' For her second baby, she chose to stay at her place. This time, her mother-in-law came to help. So did her sister. There began a long war between two generations of women over a baby. 'I was caught between fighting for my sister, asserting myself without hurting the mother-in-law and tending to the baby. It was too much! Being grounded with the frequent nursing made it even worse!'

I can't put a finger on what is tougher – carrying the baby around in you for nine months, battling bad drivers, potholed roads, mean fellow commuters and unfriendly public spaces or getting yourself together post baby. Immediately after giving birth, the preoccupation with most women seems to be to get back to their pre-pregnancy weight (and shape). Now considering that you continue to look pregnant even after giving birth (no, the stomach does not go in by elasticity), this is no mean feat and can take longer than you estimated. Unless of course you go on a raisin diet like Liz Hurley did or survive on prawns like Posh Spice. Or the still-to-be-revealed-diet of VJ Mia who loudly proclaimed that she posed in a bikini three weeks after her baby was born.

To the rest of us who don't have personal chefs, trainers, or a nanny brigade, it's tough. Sure this mega-calorie burning through breastfeeding is nature's way of helping you lose weight. But no one tells you that it also makes you so ravenous, that you end up eating twice as much anyway. Kinda self-defeating, isn't it? A few months post baby, despite enough compliments on how my body is just the same and how I don't look like I've given birth, I still felt like I was living in another person's body.

Baby Byte:
If you've gone back to size zero or whatever in six weeks, you are probably starving me.

Getting your body back is a very vague thing. It does not mean fitting into your old pair of jeans or fuck-me bra or tube dress. It means sitting down and standing up with ease, and feeling exactly the same *va va voom* you did before you were pregnant. Or being able to touch your toes and feeling exactly like you did before. Okay, just for the record: Cindy Crawford took six months to get up on her feet. You are not Cindy Crawford, you can take longer.

12
S=E=X: Where it all Started

Once upon a time, there was a boy and there was a girl. They met, fell in love, got married, had lots of noisy sex and thought they'd live happily ever after. Then they decided to have a baby. So they had intense, not-so-noisy sex for days and weeks. Until the girl announced she was pregnant. End of noisy and not-so-noisy sex.

It's true that babies can bring two people closer in the sense that it forms a completely new bond between the new parents. They just created a whole new human being, and by any standards, that's a big deal! And then, babies have this thing of being so vulnerable and need so much caring and looking after, that even if you are not a very collaborative couple, you end up doing stuff together. But it is true that it does make couples drift apart and unless you really work on intimacy, it is possible to get engrossed in baby stuff and totally forget that there is one more person to factor in. The person you made the baby with.

Funnily enough, the one thing that caused the baby to happen in the first place is the one thing that is conspicuous by its absence largely during and after pregnancy. Sex for the most part becomes a thing of low priority, both by choice and circumstance.

So pregnancy and motherhood are like a sexual sabbatical in parts. For the first three months of pregnancy, you are ridden by queasiness and lethargy and moody hormones; so you don't feel like it and are often advised by the doctor to 'take it easy'. For the next three months, you are on overdrive, because your body is ripe and voluptuous, you are in a 'good hormones' phase and generally delicious and desirable for your partner. At the pinnacle of your pregnancy, you are like a bitch on heat. You feel extra horny. You have boobs, a great body image, you are always lubricated and very easily turned on, you have good hair days and mostly feel very sexy. You also cannot get any more pregnant, so contraception is not a concern anymore. There is just one small problem. You don't get laid enough.

Plus, you want George Clooney.

My husband had issues. 'It feels...wrong! Like I am making love to my baby. Or like there is someone else in the room, watching us. And what if there's too much pressure on the baby?' I scream my lungs out. THE AMNIOTIC SAC IS IMPERVIOUS TO ORGASMIC AND OTHER SOUNDS, AND PRESSURES, DAMMIT! It didn't go down too well. Worse, me screaming like a banshee was not sexually the most attractive thing.

So while I was hot and heavy, Dee was now intimidated by the belly and the baby within. I, on the other hand, reached a point where I was ready to do it to anyone, anywhere. All those women whose husbands made love to them till the ninth month, I OFFICIALLY HATE YOU!

Baby Byte:
Don't blame me. I never said sex was banned. I can take it, you know!

When the baby pops out, the tables turn. Suddenly he is the bitch on heat and you are the one saying no. Plus, nursing and bonding with the baby supplies the feel-good hormones that sex usually provides you with, so technically, you have no use for a man for the time being. To top it all, you are so sleep deprived that any open window for sex makes you long for sleep. And you are still sore and healing and everything hurts and your body feels like it needs to be sent to a garage. Your vagina hasn't had much action in a while and might need to be lubricated with a jelly, unless you want to feel like a virgin all over again. Your breasts hurt, and any overstimulation in that area could only lead to a spurt of you-know-what. Your erogenous zones are protesting. Your G-spot has temporarily relocated to a place of unknown existence. Most importantly, where did you last put your libido?

Your liberated-from-belly body status, on the other hand, has increased your partner's libido several fold. By this time, he also realises that 'it has been a while'. The next few months are about logistics (when to do it, where to do it), technicalities (what lubrication to use) and existentialism (no time for foreplay, baby might wake up anytime, so may as well get on with it). Also, unless you are ready to have back-to-back babies, there is no room for error in the contraception department, so it takes the piss out of the sex thing for a while. Wait, there's more. He can't have sex with the baby in the room. You can't have sex with the baby in another. And should your planetary charts conspire and you do get hot and heavy, what about protection?

Our sexual rendezvous would go like this:

'Babe, you think this Saturday afternoon we could have a wild sex date?'

'Yes, I think 1 to 3 p.m. is a good window, because Re will be asleep and the maid also takes a nap.'

'Great!'

Come Saturday 1 p.m. and there would be some match on television and the husband would be three beers down and a couch potato when I would remind him of our 'sex date'.

'Oh no! May be tomorrow morning? I am really into the match now.'

'How about tonight? After the baby sleeps?'

I'm Pregnant, Not Terminally Ill, You Idiot!

'Erm...there's a Man U match at 9 p.m.'

My friend Anu used to get texts from her husband saying, 'Hoping for some bam bam tonite.' It was their code word for sex. This meant she had to get into the mood and work out the logistics by the time the husband arrived. One of their biggest deterrents was never having a condom around. She thought he should buy it and he thought it was her job. Anu and I are both petrified of Copper Ts, getting our tubes tied or having other aliens in our bodies, so contraception is still an issue we are both dealing with. Unfortunately our husbands are too alpha-male to even consider vasectomy.

Ironically, sex during pregnancy is almost spoken of as a luxury. But everyone wants you to have sex with a vengeance and make it your mission after the baby. 'Resuming your sex life' is spoken of like it's some kind of post-pregnancy anthem. As soon as you can. As much as you can. Everyone subtly and not-so-subtly eggs you to get the sex back in your life. Your mother. Your best friend. The book. The doctor (how else will he stay in business?).

The strangest bit of advice my friend Rashna ever gave me post baby was, 'Don't neglect the man. Keep the sex going. Else he will stray.'

I think Tiger Woods is to blame for this.

She also gave me a tip: 'Feed the baby *sheera* doused in ghee before bedtime. You can be sure he will be knocked out for a few hours. Use that time for sex!'

It never worked. The baby always woke up, *sheera* or no *sheera*.

The thing about sex is that no one wants to admit they are not getting enough of it. We are all supposed to be these sex machines, constantly at it, if we have a legitimate partner to have sex with and that partner is, for all practical purposes, available. So pregnancy, postpartum blues and very sleepless nights are hardly considered impediments.

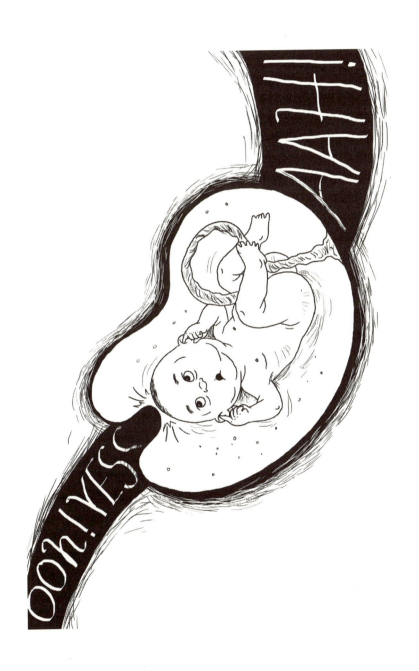

I'm Pregnant, Not Terminally Ill, You Idiot!

Even if no one is getting any, sex droughts are not something that are shared comfortably, however close your friend is to you. In fact they are only shared when another person has a story equivalent to yours in its depravity. I was telling a mommy friend how we hadn't done it in six months and she acted shocked. 'So what? We haven't done it in two years!'

But sex is the last thing on your mind after giving birth, even if it's the first thing on the husband's mind. Even dreams of the husband lap-dancing with an 'escort' didn't seem to bother me. Yes, all women suffer from a low libido postpartum (lasting from a few months to a few years), but no one talks about it. I guess it's because women want to pretend the sex goddess in them is unperturbed by all the postpartum changes in body and mind.

What does this dry period do to men? I am sure they all feel somewhat left out. Added to which is the fear of getting the woman pregnant again, keeping the sex drive at bay even more. So it's back to hand-jobs, at least for a while. And I say what's wrong with that? If women have had to do with vibrators during their pregnancy when the men were having the jitters, it only seems fair. Yes, there are women who get their libido back or manage to fake it soon enough, but if you are not one of those, do not fret.

There's also the whole fear of history repeating itself (read you getting pregnant again) and baby number two making a surprise appearance. Apparently exclusive breastfeeding for the first six months is not the natural contraceptive it is made out to be, and there have been 'accidents' and 'oops babies'. So it's back to having sex like singletons – like bring on the condom, bring on the pill, the diaphragm, the IUD, whatever works for you.

Of course, if you don't have issues with tandem nursing, or losing the four hours of sleep that you would normally get, well go for it and have sex like rabbits. Else, go back to keeping a menstrual diary and pray that the ovulation gods don't strike again.

This time around, the sex needs more work, more planning for sure. If there is the drive and the inclination, your body may not be on your side. Sleepless nights play havoc with your sprightliness, and therefore your moves could be quite rusty, and might need practice. What certainly helps in rekindling your sex life is a change of scene, or a spontaneous date with your husband just like the old times. A quick weekend getaway might do the trick. Minus baby would be better, if you can manage to pump enough in advance for his feeds. You can pretend to be canoodling singletons, or do the jazz, wine and candles bit, cuddle, watch a movie and take it from there. Of course, provided you have someone to take charge of the baby. Unfortunately, alcohol cannot be employed as a suitable aphrodisiac if you are nursing the baby. So you may have to improvise. Pretend your strawberries are doused in champagne. Or get drunk on half a glass of wine.

Your new sleeping arrangements often serve as a barometer of your sex life...at least for the beholder. It seems to be the popular notion that if your baby is sleeping with you, you are probably not getting any. A friend of mine knew we were still co-sleeping with our son. She asked me, 'So what does that do to your sex life?'

What they really want to know is 'How long has the dry period been?'

Others are more subtle. 'So, do you and Dee get time together? You know what I mean?'

Yes I do, and it's none of your business.

Personally, I don't buy into the notion of 'three is a crowd' post baby, at least where sex is concerned. Honestly, does any one of us have any memory of sexual acts between our parents before we were three? That says it all. What the baby doesn't know about doesn't hurt the baby (or you), so what difference does that make? And how has any child been permanently scarred by watching his parents making love or getting intimate? The bottom line is, if you and your partner are really feeling hot and heavy, there is no baby, no crib, no sleeping arrangement that can really be a deterrent. We've all had our share of sneak peeks, so may the tradition continue.

13

Maid in Heaven

Here's a bit of advice. If you are planning to get pregnant, visit your family tree to find out if there is an old aunt, grandmother, cousin of a grandmother or grandmother of a cousin who might have the potential or be kind enough to bequeath a domestic help to you, before you even start plotting your ovulation calendar. Having found this person, use all your charm to ensure you have her on your side, give her regular updates about your pregnancy, buy her little gifts from time to time, pose for pictures with her and send her laminated copies, so that you always sit on her bedside table, reminding her of the fact that you exist.

You will realise that investing in some good family PR before the baby comes, can go a long way in finding that elusive, precious, worth-her-weight-in-gold entity. The baby-maid. Because she will be the one person who can make life easier for you when the baby pops out. In your scheme of things, she will be far more valuable than the husband, mother and mother-in-law put together (there's a lot of rocking, walking, changing, burping, feeding, wheeling, running after to do). If you don't do this, or are less fortunate, it might take you months, years to find a baby-maid who'd work for you.

Baby Byte:
If your friend knows a good maid,
why didn't she hire her?

I'm Pregnant, Not Terminally Ill, You Idiot!

The perfect maid is like the perfect man. She doesn't exist. Think about it this way and you won't feel as miserable. What you should do is work around the one you have, however imperfect, and bring her up to a level that suits you. At least for the time being. Year zero to two is the toughest, and maids are at a premium here. So while babies may be the gift of God, it is the maids who are finally made in heaven. If you find someone borderline good, do anything to keep her. If you haven't, well, God bless you!

As if it's not enough that you feel like a complete imbecile struggling to get your life together post baby, there will be opinions from all quarters on the baby-maid and how to find this person. Advice will come pouring from one and all:

'Tell your watchman, milkman, istriwala. You never know.'

'Why don't you go to the nearest church? I believe all churches offer a maid-service.'

'What about an NGO?'

'Why don't you ask your mother?'

'Ask your mother-in-law.'

'What about your driver? Maybe he has a wife. Or a daughter. Or sister.'

'Just get a girl from the village and train her.'

'Spread the word. Tell everyone you know.'

'Why don't you ask your cook or cleaning lady if she wants a promotion? It will be extra income for her.'

Probably the only real piece of wisdom I ever got about maids was from my friend Anjali. She believed in 'hire and fire'. 'There is no time to interview, scrutinise and test-run them. So just hire anyone who comes your way and fire them if they don't work out. This way your life will not come to a stand-still.' She must have hired and fired at least ten maids by the time her daughter was two. Her logic? 'Never look for a perfect maid, she doesn't exist. Look for someone who needs the job. She will always do for now.' It's a bit warped, but it works.

The only qualification for a good maid is that she should be able to join you the very next day. Because, if you have a baby and no help, sometimes, the only reason to hire a maid is that she is available.

Which means you are spared the agony of 'Will she or won't she show up?' If she does show up, you will figure out in the first two days whether she is worth training or investing in, or whether you should continue the hunt for another one and then sack the first when the second one shows up. Which is what Anjali did, with no qualms.

My two-bit addendum to the Anjali philosophy is also to set very low benchmarks. Like factoring in her availability for just a month. If she is the 'not dependable' type, she will disappear a few days after she is paid her first month's salary. No maid ever 'quits' or gives you the real reason for quitting and that is something you should know. She just goes away and never comes back. So stop dialling that number.

Baby Byte:
If the baby maid quits, it's not me, it's you!

Of course the ones who are truly chicken leave by day three (it has happened to me twice) and don't give a damn about getting paid because all they want is to get the hell out of your life and your baby's. If she lasts ten days, she will usually last a month. Leaving in ten would mean not getting paid, so you are sorted for month one. Now the challenge is to start working your charms around her for month two and make her last another month. Then another. Then another. Until she truly wants to stay.

I'm Pregnant, Not Terminally Ill, You Idiot!

Some extremely finicky parents claim they interviewed ten maids before settling on the eleventh, as none were good enough for their child. Well, I think they are lying. Try asking them to pass you the numbers of the earlier ten and notice how they will dither and eventually disappear.

Then there is the whole strategy of recruiting live-ins, as opposed to day maids, although beggars can't be choosers and I clearly was a beggar. It is true that a live-in gives you more recovery time and perhaps enough notice to hire a replacement, as there are logistics involved. She lives with you, is perhaps from another city/village, so has to find a job, move her stuff, things like that. You could perhaps use this time to egg her on to stay on or offer her a raise, additional perks, your makeup or keys to your car. If you consider the time and effort you will spend training another one, it's worth it. Or you could meet other maids on the sly while she is still around. Even though most flats, at least in Bombay, barely have enough space for you and the baby, it seems to be smarter to hire a live-in than a day-maid.

But here again, I realised, a contingency plan is important. Perhaps the most terrible thing to happen to you other than a colicky baby is a baby-maid quitting without notice. This is a catastrophe that causes your entire workflow to collapse. Food can be ordered, dishes can be done, floors can be mopped by anyone, but looking after a baby is a full-time job and cannot be done by just about anyone. It requires skills of a very convoluted nature, some of which I still haven't mastered.

I then realised that, forget the maids, even you haven't come pre-trained for baby-care. It's your first time, too, and we all learn as we go.

Baby Byte:
Yes, it's a shit job. But someone has to do it.

For a few months, when finding someone half-decent was looking impossible to me, I tried to be one of those martyr moms who 'did everything herself'. I realised quite soon how difficult it was to do basic things like have a bath, eat, pee, answer the doorbell with my boob in my infant's mouth. Forget doing complicated things like having a phone conversation, checking email and other stuff. It's all very overwhelming and depleting of your already low energy. And how many nappies can you change really?

In case you are still wondering why are there such few takers for baby-maid jobs, the reasons are many and each one is as bizarre as the other. Primarily it is because no one wants to do the dirty work. Maids find it easier to freelance, that is do a series of odd jobs that add up to a tidy sum, rather than be 'stuck' in one job that pays them relatively less and robs them of their freedom. It's like committing to one guy (that too, a clingy one) when you can date several.

And even if you are willing to pay them the upper end of the salary bracket, it would still be easier for them to make as much money by splitting it up across various cooking and cleaning jobs than being a baby-maid. So the only reason someone would want to be a baby maid is because she really likes you or the baby or needs a place to stay.

Think about this. A baby-maid has to change nappies, sometimes as many as twenty times a day. That makes it at least twice in every wakeful hour. Then she has to talk to a baby that does not talk back to her. And that too in a language she has to

make up as she goes. Then she has to bathe, feed, walk, rock, burp the baby, walk it around in its pram or stroller, pretending to be deeply interested in the baby's cooings. Then she has to pick up everything the baby drops, be drooled, peed on, sometimes have her hair pulled, face rearranged, food messed with. After all that, the baby will jump at its mother the minute he spots her and pretend that the baby-maid never really existed.
It's hard.

Let's begin with me. I never thought I had any trouble in the retaining power department of domestics. I had never sacked anyone. No one had sacked me. Until the baby happened.

My baby-maid adventure

Baby-maids. Well trained and fully hands-on. So said the ad on the wall at Breach Candy Hospital. I decided I had no choice but to give it a shot, because between asking the cleaning lady to extend her hours and the cook to babysit once in a while when I had to run an errand, I had no other help once I was back home from the hospital.

I called the number on the ad.

Day one. Someone who looked like a cross between a paan-chewing thug and a fisherwoman appeared. Now I am not a snob, but when you have a baby that's a few days old, you are a little finicky about who picks him up and what olfactory treats it's exposed to. Anyway, you never know, I thought and figured I should give it a try.

The first thing she did was start undressing. Right in the middle of my living room! I was aghast and suddenly wondered if she had come to the right address for the right job and asked her what she was doing. She quickly pulled out another sari from a small plastic bag she was carrying and announced, 'I am changing into work clothes.'

Phew!

And she was only one of many. There was one that tried to change the baby's nappy while it was still in the crib, soaking in its pee. There was one that wandered off to find a wipe while leaving the one-month-old precariously at the edge of the cot. Both were fired in a day. They scooted off without a blink.

There was another one that spoke only Telugu, a language I did not speak or understand. The best thing about her was that she was straight off the boat, as raw as they come. I was ecstatic that there was no unlearning for her to do and I could mould her any way I liked. My joy was short-lived as I soon found out she was infested with head-lice and spread the epidemic to everyone in the household, including the baby. I doused her and the rest of the household with anti-lice shampoo for the next few days. Evidently her crop was far more abundant than ours and wouldn't really yield. I was at my wit's end. I asked her to take a week off and do something, anything to get rid of the lice. She came back, a week later, stark raving bald. *At least she is committed*, I thought, feeling pleased that I had finally found one who would last. She did. For four months. She got homesick after and wanted to go back to her village.

I was desperate. I called a maid agency. 'I need a baby-maid for a nine-month-old. Like, tomorrow.' They called back within ten minutes. 'Yes, there is a girl. She is very pleasant, can speak a bit of English, has excellent references, is very good for baby work, and plus, she can also cook.' She sounded good enough to marry. I said yes. He said, 'Okay, she will be at your place tomorrow at 9 a.m., and my man will be there with her file of documents.'

I'm Pregnant, Not Terminally Ill, You Idiot!

Now this is where the scam starts (and the sleuth in me found this out after a casual chat with one of the potential candidates). What I learnt from her was that anyone and everyone who shows up at the agency's door is pitched within the next one hour to desperate moms looking for maids. The 'file' that they refer to contains one item – a photocopy of her ration card.

The catch is, once you hire a girl from the agency, you are liable to pay them one month's salary (the designated salary amount is laid down for all maids they promote, irrespective of the fact that the said maid has never held a baby, leave alone been a baby-maid for someone else). Once the cash is in their bag, and God forbid the maid turns out to be a disaster, you will be chasing them for days for a replacement. They will of course, say they 'will call you back' and you will still be waiting for that call.

I hired one. She was okay, except for the fact that she spoke more on her phone than to me or the baby. Also, once she napped, even a tsunami couldn't wake her, forget a crying baby. I had to let her go. I am still waiting for that replacement.

Then there are pimps or one-woman agencies, like this Ms Ghosh I met. She claimed she 'got girls' every day. Each time I called her or she gave me one of her famous 'missed calls', she would say, 'Yes, one girl is arriving by the next train, and I can bring her tomorrow.' Or, 'One girl has just arrived and is sitting right next to me and I can bring her now if you pay me the taxi-fare.' One would imagine that she lived in this palatial house which provided shelter to the homeless, but it turned out that her so-called office was a room in a chawl. She had the same glowing accolades for every girl, however little she knew her.

Obviously her agenda was clear – how to get these women who had sought her through references, out of her one-room mansion as soon as possible. The plan was fool-proof. She would bring the girl with a story well rehearsed. The girl is always 'very good at her work', even though she has never dressed or bathed a baby, and can barely tell the right side of a diaper. If you hemmed and hawed, she would say, 'Please decide fast, otherwise I will offer the maid to the next party.' By this time you have panicked so much, that you say yes to everything. You of course had to pay for her transport and the 2000 rupee commission upfront, so you would have no bargaining power left.

I hired one.

She fired me.

She left on day two. It seems she didn't like my bathroom.

I was maidless in Bombay again.

Ms Ghosh never returned my calls.

The husband and I were now at a loss for how to win our maids over. He came up with a strategy. 'Let's just up their salary and give them as little work as possible.' It didn't make any sense to me. My strategy was to make them feel that they could be worse off elsewhere. That I am a better boss than anyone else they can find.

'Just get two maids, and one will keep an eye on the other,' my ever-so-wise friend Rama advised.

'Yes, but can I get one first?'

I did eventually get two (divine intervention), but other than the shock of huge grocery and milk bills, I had the added peeve of figuring out how to keep them busy and how not to make them delegate work internally, so that one always got the short end of the stick.

Look at my life. Month zero till month four. No baby-maid. Month five to month ten. Baby-maid one. Month ten-twelve. No maid. Month twelve. Baby-maid two. Month thirteen. No maid. Month fourteen. Baby-maid three and four. Month fifteen till twenty. Baby-maid five. Month twenty till date. Maidless.

By month eight, I had reached a point where I would even steal a maid, if I could. Poaching was hugely on my mind and any place I visited that used service staff – like a day-care centre, the local beauty parlour, the doctor's clinic, I would quickly eye the women staff and picture them being all tender and loving towards my baby. I would quickly compute their salary and try to make them an offer, always to be rejected, because everyone thought baby-work was too much *magachmaari* (pain-in-the-ass-work). Also, like the builder mafias, the maid mafia ensures that all maids are paid on par, so there is no question of usurping, because if people find out you are paying more than the market rates, well, you will be blacklisted. No one will ever give you any phone numbers. Because your maid will tell their maid who will tell the world and soon the maids will be on strike and everyone will blame you. So whatever you do, do it discreetly.

To cut and keep:

How to get a maid in ten days

However impossible or onerous the task of finding a baby-maid seems to be, there are a few leads that can help you get somewhere. This is how you can systematically go about finding a baby-maid:

Ancestral legacies

Inherit one. What are parents and in-laws for? In fact I think, the best thing your mother/mother-in-law can ever do for you is pass on her legacy of a cook or maid who will live with you and look after you and your child forever and ever. Or at least till you need her. If a mother-in-law is looking to earn brownie points, she has hit the jackpot with this one. As for the mother, if she has one, she is yours anyway.

Maid agencies

These are shadier-than-thou and also demand a brokerage. They are of different types and sizes and efficiencies (like the few I described). Some are hole-in-the-wall establishments, with an office, a desk and someone manning it; some operate from home; and some have no fixed address. They all charge a commission, which varies from a month's salary to a third of a month's salary, payable on joining and non-refundable if the maid doesn't work out. Of course, they all promise a replacement, should such an unforeseen thing happen, but they seldom deliver on that.

Churches

Did you know that a few churches in the city have a special mass service (in a vernacular language) for domestic helps? That this is almost like a maid buffet, except that you are not on the buffet and will therefore stand out? I actually stood outside the church down the lane a few Sundays in a row, with a wad of post-its with my name and number on it, handing them out to every girl who passed by. In fact, I even took three of them home over a period of two weeks. I even got one to quit her existing job and convinced her that looking after a baby looked better on her résumé than managing a house (which she was doing). It took her forty-eight hours to learn that it was not.

Friends

I have known people who have stolen their friends' baby-maids by dangling bigger carrots. Everything seems to be fair in baby and war, and I was close to doing this, till I had a windfall of a maid.

Parks, building complexes, lifts

For months, I strutted around every evening at 5 p.m. in my neighbourhood, smartly dressed and perfumed, each day picking a different building or block, and while I wheeled my baby around in his stroller, I kept a hawk's eye for every nanny/maid that seemed open to the idea of infidelity. The things you do when you are desperate!

How to lose a maid in ten days

- Take her to a friend's place. A friend more affluent, living in a better neighbourhood, who has a more respectable pin code than yours, serves more meat than you ever did, whose maids are ferried around by their drivers in posher cars than yours and who has a retinue of maids in lieu of your one.
- Have more off-limits areas, foods or activities in your house than she can handle. If she is constantly told, 'Don't do this' or 'Don't open that' or 'Don't eat that', she is going to want out soon. Using your face caviar and eating your crème brûlée is a no-no. But one should turn a blind eye to a fruit here, a cheesecake there or a TV show every once in a while.
- Try and optimise her by adding on bits of 'other work' that strictly doesn't fall under the purview of baby work. Like cooking, cleaning, paying utility bills, ironing curtains, walking the dog. STICK TO THE BABY!
- Forget to tell her one nice thing a few minutes after you accidentally reprimanded her.
- Exclude her from family dos or eat too much of the good stuff and not share with her.
- Not let her make contact with her family whenever she needs to.

I'm Pregnant, Not Terminally Ill, You Idiot!

- Forget to thank her for something thoughtful that she may have done.
- Not reward her for her pro-activeness.
- Tell her that she eats too much.

14

Sisterhood of the Wailing Mommies

There is a certain kind of woman you never want to be when you become a mother. The kind whose world revolves around her baby, the kind who cannot have a single conversation without references to her child (how cute he is, what word did she say today, what milestone he is at), the kind who cancels on you because her baby has passed an extra motion, the kind who's always whining about public places being so baby-unfriendly, the kind who starts preparing excel sheets for playgroups, nurseries and schools that she would like to send her baby to, the kind whose vocabulary begins and ends with babyisms.

Unlike singledom, where you can pick and choose your friends or marriage, where you inherit some, pick some, motherhood is about union by circumstance or happenstance. You just happened to be at the same place at the same time – a pre or postnatal yoga class, the ob-gyn's reception area, the bed next door at the hospital, a La Leche League meeting, wheeling your baby at the park, attending a mother-toddler program, playgroup, music class, baby gym, whatever – and that's reason enough for you to be on each other's speed-dial.

Now, there is also union through adversity. Anyone who has the same issues as you is also your new best friend. So you could bond over postpartum depression, engorged breasts, over-intrusive in-laws, loneliness, feeling left out of the rat race, the search for the elusive maid, husbands who tremble every time they have to hold the baby, couch potato husbands or husbands who are dead to the world while the baby shrieks in the middle of the night.

Whatever the bonding factor, there is only one thing a woman needs to know when she calls another in the first few months after child birth. Are you as miserable as she is? If not, you will soon be off her list. You don't like to hear that someone else's life is sorted when you are struggling with yours, do you? However, listening to another person's misery could be cathartic and make you count your blessings.

So if you have a maid problem, she better have a maid problem. If you have a paranoid cutlet for a mother, she better not have one of those chilled-out moms. If you have mother-in-law issues, she better not have a cool mother-in-law. If your baby keeps you up all night, hers had better not be a blissful eight-hour sleeper. If you have trouble getting your husband to be more hands-on, she better not have one of those husbands who are happy to carry the baby as long as you want, rock him to sleep, feed him dinner, bathe him. And definitely not say things like, 'I want to watch Formula One. Can I be off baby duty?'

The conversations before and after the baby are like fantasy vs reality. When you are pregnant, you are calling to share the buoyancy, hear affirmations, share secrets and tips. It's all about the good stuff – is it kicking, how often are you eating, what are your cravings, how big have your boobs become – stuff like that. Every pregnant woman has a pregnant buddy, someone who has been there just before her, who is always one step ahead of her, so she can learn from her mistakes.

Soon after I became a mother, I had pregnant women calling me all the time, just to get things off their system. They weren't looking for answers or advice. It didn't matter what I said or felt; all they wanted was to be heard.

Baby Byte:
We are not the problem. We just do as we are told to do. It's the mommies who need fixing.

Post baby, the conversations are as varied as why is the child not feeding from the right breast and how do I make him sleep better at night, what is the best way to wear the baby, what to do with engorged breasts or overwhelming mothers, and what to do for visual stimulation.

Strangely, most of the women who will now be part of your comfort zone will be the women you always dreaded hanging out with. For one, they can't talk about anything other than baby issues. They don't read the same books, listen to the same music, have the same wicked take on stuff, dig the same food, same films, same men. Oh well, you are as different as chalk and cheese. Deal with it!

And yet...

- You can have a perfectly normal conversation with them.
- You end up calling them for information on nannies, day-cares, play schools, toy libraries, mother-toddler programs, potty training, sleep rituals, recipes.
- You always find an excuse to meet them.
- You are willing to overlook all their eccentricities.

Baby Byte:
I think mommy has some strange friends. Now, if only I don't have to be friends with their babies.

Something has obviously shifted in your universe. It is amazing how much your scope of conversation changes. Suddenly, diaper logistics, vaccination theories, baby-related activity, child-friendly restaurants, changing stations, car seats and nannies become the centre of your universe. This will graduate to play groups, playdates, daycare, schools and activity centres and go on to projects, PTA meetings and whatnots.

So here are my new best friends:

The 'My-daughter-is-so-naughty-I-have-never-seen-her-sit-in-one place' mom

These are the types who take pride in an over-frisky, precocious child who is usually wont to shrieking like a banshee for no apparent reason, beating up any random man/woman/child/animal that it can get its hands on, and running amuck in a public place. They celebrate the fact that the child is 'so free' that it's hard to pin down. My cherub would religiously get shoved and pushed by one such hyperactive child in the park. And his mother would never cease to be amazed.

The 'What-do-I-feed-the-child?' mom

These are the culinarily challenged mommies who even hundreds of baby-toddler cookbooks cannot redeem. They are always at a loss for how to make kiddie food more interesting and can only go as far as adding ketchup or cheese to everything. So they are constantly moaning about the fact that the child doesn't eat. Or are figuring out what to make for breakfast, lunch, dinner, snacks, what to pack in the baby bag and such like.

The 'Where-has-my-life-gone?' mom

These are women who are initially so overcome by motherhood that they give up pursuing all their other goals, professional or personal, get out of the race, start living on the me-and-my-baby island, and then one fine day, when they feel chained and ensnared by the babydom thing, moan that they have no life left.

The 'I-want-a-job-where-I-can-be-home-at-4 p.m.-for-my-girls-and-get-paid-fabulously' mom

This once-corporate-honcho-now-full-time mom type cannot come to terms with the fact that she has been left behind in the race, despite her Ivy League degree. While she is making a career of being an excel-sheet mom, her contemporaries are busy appearing on television, becoming corporate honchos, winning awards or writing books. But now that the babies are all grown up and don't need her the way they used to, she is bereft and suddenly on a I-have-to-get-my-life-back mission.

The 'I-am-having-a-blast-being-a-mom' type

I actually saw this on the Google chat status message of a fellow mom who had given birth two months ago. Granted mommyhood could be many things to many people, but blast? I would designate them as the wannabe cool mommies who think saying such things will move them up in the hierarchy of cool moms. They actually go into orgasms whenever the words 'milestone' or 'visual stimulation' or some such is mentioned. The said mommy has since disappeared from my radar.

The 'I-don't-care-what-I-look-like-or-what-I-wear' type

These are the totally selfless, baby-obsessed mothers whose entire being is about how to make the baby the centre of their lives while turning into a wallflower themselves. 'Let me forget about what I wear or what I look like, because who is interested in me? I have no problems being the sack lady. Isn't everyone looking at the baby anyway?'

No, my dear, they are looking at you and wondering what will become of the baby's dress sense in a few months. Perhaps one reason why you wouldn't mind hanging out with such wardrobe-malfunctioned moms is because they make you look good.

The 'When-will-I-be-size-zero-again?' mom

These are moms that monitored every microgram of their pregnancy and now, post baby, have already enrolled for all the crash weight-loss and baby-fat-knockoff programs, tummy tucks and whatever they can get, so that they can go shopping for size-zero clothes again. Or fit into their old ones.

The paranoid, antiseptic NRI mom

This one pre-orders Pampers Dry Baby in bulk before coming to India and would even contemplate carrying water all the way from America on her annual visit to India. She actually believes that the water we drink would affect the oesophageal reflexes of her child. She would go as far as emailing the head of marketing at Kimberley Clarke on why her brand of Pampers is not available in India.

The 'I-am-not-a-hypochondriac-just-careful' mom

This one is a pharmacist's delight. She believes every condition needs a cure and she is a panacea. So at the drop of a hat, she will pump her baby with nasal drops, Crocin syrup, homeopathic medicines to speed teething, medicines to soothe the gums while the said teeth come out, and medicines to make her sleep while she agonises over the pain of teething. And of course, vitamins. Plenty of them. In later years, such mothers are prone to give memory drugs, drugs to aid digestion, promote better appetites, increase height, intelligence and other such.

The 'I-love-my-son-so-much-I can't-bear-to-let-anyone-touch-him' mom

These are the types who refuse to delegate or outsource any of the baby duty (good, bad, downright dirty) and insist on taking it all upon themselves. Yes, we all go through fleeting phases of 'no maid is good enough' for my baby before practicality takes over or before we learn to lower our benchmarks. But some mothers are afflicted by this forever.

The 'I-am-so-dying-to-party-and-have-tequila-shots' mom

My friend Jenny was always calculating exactly at what point between breastfeeds could she have a drink. I guess the baby was hampering her hedonistic lifestyle and she was dying to break free and get it all together. The last I saw her, she had joined a power yoga class, had a nutritionist and a trainer, and wanted to know when she could start weaning. The baby was three months old and already on solids.

Lalita Iyer

The 'What-class-does-your-child-go-for?' mom

This hyperactive and secretly bored mommy is living out her dreams through her child, packing his life with as much activity and learning as she possibly can, and then pretending it was the baby who asked for it or needed it. So if it's Monday, it must be music, Tuesday – art, Wednesday – puppetry, Thursday – karate, Friday – Math for geniuses, Saturday – GK, Sunday – gymnastics. If she could fit in gardening and taekwondo into his schedule, she would.

One park-mommy friend wanted to know, 'So are you sending him anywhere?' I reckoned she meant my son, so I mumbled and fumbled and I said, 'Well, we go to parks, the beach, play-dates, music class, markets, the library, long drives.'

She was not impressed. She said she found the music class repetitive and monotonous and her child was not learning anything. She had just enrolled him for GK and phonetics instead. He had just turned three.

The micro-label-analysers

One of my fellow mommies was a self-appointed nutrition fanatic who believed that anything and everything off-the-shelf or pre-packaged is harmful to the baby. She would quickly compute the percentage of hydrogenated fat or preservatives in a packet of biscuits or peanut butter and convince you that unless you grow everything in your backyard, nothing is worthy of consumption. She had no problem with formula though.

The 'It's-four-o'clock-so-it's-visual-stimulation-time' mom

I know a little bit of discipline never hurt anyone, but these schedule-obsessed moms are something else. Perhaps it starts with 'ten minutes on each breast', or 'bath time 11 a.m.', or 'mashed apple at 4 p.m.' and 'bird watching at 5 p.m.' or 'blowing bubbles at 6 p.m.' or 'listening to nursery rhymes at 7 p.m.'

The '*My-daughter-is-now-into-twelve-word-sentences*' mom

A fellow mommy at the park (okay, you meet a lot of them) would give me an update on her daughter every time we met. She always used the royal personal pronoun, which I found amusing. 'We are now speaking in twelve-word sentences. We are now eating on our own. We are now drinking water from a glass like grown-ups.'

When I first told my friend Rama that I couldn't believe I was friends with all these weirdos, all she said was, 'There is more to come. Just grin and bear it. You have no idea what kind of women will be at the centre of your universe in a year or two.'

Since I was a stay-at-home mommy, I guess by default I was around the baby most of the time, hence the probability of having weirdo friends is higher. My working-mommy counterparts, like my friend Mandira, have other dilemmas. 'I never know what's going on, because I hardly hang out with other moms. I feel as though I live in a parallel universe. No one tells me anything.'

The people you will really miss are your single friends. Post baby, single women will shift out of your radar for a while as your preoccupations are so different from theirs. You don't care about the new hotspots or their man problems or what did they shop for in Hong Kong, so you have very little to say or do with them. Also, the dynamic has changed between you and your single girlfriends. You now represent the womb. It's a reminder of their biological clocks, the pressure of finding a suitable man to make a baby with, or the pressure of getting married. Unless the single woman has abundant empathy or baby-sitting potential, you may not be bonding much, at least in the first two years. But this is just a phase, and if they hang in there, they can have you back, and you will be just as good as when they left you.

Baby Byte:
Actually I don't mind the whiners as much as the
cheek pinchers.

Another thing I discovered, and this is true of most women, is that we all have different girlfriends to fill different voids – one girlfriend who is a problem fixer, one who we can moan about our husbands to, one for in-law bitching, one for domestic issues, one for cerebral parenting, one for work, career and other issues, one for body, fashion and retail therapy, one for soul, one for relationship politics, one for how-to and one for why-does-this-happen. There is never a one-size-fits-all.

A true friend at this point is one who never offers a quick fix to any problem, rather she hears you out (however long it takes), empathises, nods, makes all the right sounds and only offers advice when asked. The best thing a friend can do is to agree that your problems are real.

Sometimes, all you need is one person you can be your most uncensored, sad, whiny self with, because that is really important for therapy – to get all the poison out. I had made a pact with my friend Neha that we were free to use each other anytime of day or night for the whiniest, bitchiest, outpourings. But we extracted a promise from each other that our whining will not be repeated to anyone else – it might just make us look less cool than we appeared to be.

It's no wonder then that new mothers hate to be around those divas who seem to have their whole life in order – whether it's work, domestic or social life – with their trainer-chef-nanny brigade, while you are struggling with just holding on to a maid or finding one. It is not supposed to happen that way, and anyone who does a better job of it than you is utterly despicable.

For me, the sign of a cool mommy is someone who does motherhood with a sense of humour and doesn't get overly militant about everything. I really looked up to my friend Iris. She was never an over-the-top mommy, didn't speak about her son unless specifically asked, still went out with the girls, managed to balance her baby and job and never made it look like a crusade. And if I ever had a question to ask, she would always have practical advice, but she never sounded like she knew it all, although she did.

With men, it's much simpler. They are just blissed out by fatherhood and have no idea of the looming politics behind it all. And when did men ever need a connection for friendship? The fact that someone else drinks beer or watches football is enough cause for bonding.

15

What Does Baby Do Now?

1

'Are you reading to your child? I read to her when she was still in my belly. Now she is five months and goes to sleep with her book.'

'My son knew all his nursery rhymes by the time he was two.'

'My daughter can recognise all the animals in the book.'

'I played classical music every day. It's great for developing their math faculty. My son is just three and he already knows numbers from one to hundred.'

Yes, good for you. But what will he do when he is eight? Derivatives?

Sorry, but mommies showing off baby milestones just make me retch. It almost feels like you are taking credit for someone else's work.

Whatever you may think, or no matter how many books you read, babies are always ahead of you. By the time you have got your act together about baby basics – what to pack in the baby bag, what to do when the baby throws a tantrum halfway into a car ride when you are the only person in the car, how to change a baby in the car without giving yourself or the baby a nervous breakdown, what to do with engorged breasts – it's time for baby milestones.

Poor babies! They don't even know that long before they are born, they are being mapped. Are they kicking well, moving their hands enough, sleeping in the right position? Are they fluttering, do they sleep when they are meant to sleep, play when they are meant to play? Right from how he or she is born to how well he or she latches on, how much does she cry, how many feeds does she take, how many times did it take for her to produce canary yellow potty, it's performance anxiety from the word go!

Ever heard women compare notes about the 'kicks'? That is where it all starts.

'Oh, mine kicks like a football player.'
'Really? I can hardly feel any movement.'

Then there is the whole birth-weight business
'So what was her birth-weight?'
'2.5 kg.'
'Mine was huge. 3.6 kg!'

When mothers meet, they inadvertently exchange notes on whether their child is turning, sitting, teething, crawling, standing, walking, or talking.

'So is he walking?'
'Not really, but with support, yes…'
'Is he talking?'
'Not yet, but he is just fifteen months.'
'Mine started talking at eleven months!'

I was part of this pro natural-birth network where women exchanged information and experiences on birthing, lactation, pre- and postnatal health and everything mommy and baby. I was shocked by the number of queries posted by members on 'How to provide the best stimulation to babies to improve creativity/cognitive skills.' It seemed a bit ironic for someone to intervene so much with the baby's development after strongly advocating the natural path.

Once the child starts crawling and moving about, the parental units are usually left tearing their hair about 'how to provide visual stimulation'. This is no mean feat, because unlike a movie or a circus or a magic show, this has to be done pretty much 24x7 (barring the few hours the baby spends sleeping).

Babies have a lot of time. This despite the fact that they take a couple of naps, go for a walk (either in their strollers or on their own twos) at least once a day, eat five to six meals a day, bathe, poop and pee a lot, and change more often than you. They still have enough time left. Filling a baby's day with activities is harder than you think. A single day for the baby is hundreds of five-minute pockets (that's the threshold of baby's attention span for anything other than sleep). How to fill those millions of pockets, is something you simply have to figure out 'on the go'. No matter how many books you read or online forums you are a part of or activity centres you line up to, there will be plenty of room left for more. Babies have an insatiable appetite for raising the bar. So it is not about having a plan B, but a plan C and D as well.

Baby Byte:
How about getting down on all fours and seeing things from our perspective? Do you realise how big everything looks from where we are?

The thing is, babies aren't really looking to you for ideas. They are quite content and can't be bothered really. Think of the possibilities. A pail of water. Half hour. Playing with their food. Half hour. Rearranging their toys, books, clothes, your face, anything – half hour. Staring from the window – fifteen minutes. Talking to the cat (mine did this) – fifteen minutes. Random walking/crawling around the house, picking up interesting objects – half hour. Putting said object in the mouth – thirty seconds. Pretending said object doesn't exist when you try to prise it out – twenty minutes. Sweeping/mopping the house – half hour. Trailing the maid – twenty minutes. Playing with pots and pans in the kitchen – half hour. Peering into

fridge, cupboard, linen closet, book case, any place they don't have unsupervised access to – forever!

Not that babies care, but your motherly wisdom compounded by some utterly redundant baby books will want you to get involved. You then realise how a perfectly innocuous activity takes forever. You forget you have to map it in baby time. No wonder, days seem inordinately long when you are with a baby.

You are advised the following:

'Read to the baby.'

'Sing songs. Dance. Perform.'

'Make funny faces.'

'Provide different visual stimuli.'

You may feel that the baby is doing fairly okay without you doing any of the above, but now, something has been triggered. Are you being a good mother? Are you doing enough? Are you providing enough stimuli?

If you plot it in real time, you will realise how much work it is reading to a baby for even fifteen minutes. In baby time, five minutes is like an hour. Go figure! And if you sit down to read or play with the child, you will realise just how much time one just whiles away and is not accounted for. For a child, a day is like a week, and it comprises several parts, each of which it expects something out of, and wants to play an active role in.

Baby Byte:
Forget the books. Read the baby.

Of course, if you are one of those super-cool parents who has spent the first half of their lives majoring in courses on child rearing or creating visual aids for babies, this may be very easy. But since most of us spent our early years chasing careers to make a living, pay EMIs, or be able to afford babies, etc., this becomes a mighty challenge.

Everyone starts off well. Pointing to crows and pigeons (or whatever wildlife is available in their urban jungle), spinning stories around them, taking them to the park, pointing in the direction of various flora and fauna. Since I don't live in National Geographic or Animal Planet land and since my city is in possession of a zoo where most of the animals are terminally ill, too old or just drugged, there is not much in terms of wildlife and animal beauty that I can offer him. Except my own cats and the local stray dogs.

With more baby books, comes the over emphasis for visual stimuli. Which goes to exaggerated lengths and provides fat incomes to baby-mother programs, baby gyms, music classes, toy manufacturers, book publishers, toy libraries, play schools and activity centres. I guess the entire business model of toymakers, baby activity centres and mother-baby programs is based on your low threshold for baby handling and limited baby vocabulary and high possibility of wishing to delegate. So whether it is the park mommy who sent her child to phonetics class or my friend Ritu who sent her daughter to play school at fifteen months or Shagorika whose son learnt what a dust-pan is in his GK class – it's all about delegation.

Principally, what wisdom teaches us is that babies are easily bored and distracted and hence look for something new to do every time. Now whether it is an old washcloth that he takes a fancy to or an IQ-enhancing toy that costs Rs 3999, the baby doesn't really give a damn.

The books and baby websites may tell you otherwise, but my suggestion is to first hear it from the baby. When the baby is ready to play, it will tell you so. When it's ready to walk, talk, sing, dance, it will make sure you are the first to know. And no baby is eager to learn nursery rhymes, or how to count from one to ten or the alphabet, or the colours of the rainbow, so you may as well leave that for the school.

I decided to follow my instinct, and did whatever felt right. But I was often confronted by milestone-vomiting mommies. Like the one who told me, 'Guess what, my daughter is speaking twelve-word sentences!'

'Wow! That must sound great!'
'What about your son? He must be talking now too...'
'Well, he says mama and dada...'
'That's all?'

It was enough to drive me ecstatic. But her comment bothered me. Maybe I was not doing enough? I tried all the 'book stuff'. When I chose to read to him, all he wanted was to rip the book off my hand and focus on me instead. I was shocked. Shouldn't he be imbibing all my glorious reading genes and start reading at age five months? No such luck. Books were mere props for him or things to be thrown on the floor to get my quick attention. Sometimes they also made for good pillows.

I thought he needed more. Performance, maybe? I beamed in wonderment, rolling my eyes and producing what I thought was innovative voices, reading *Mouse Soup Stories*, *Where is Baby's Belly Button?* and *Puss in Boots*. He was not amused. Although I must admit that he expressed a marginal interest in the baby's feet, which were hidden behind the cat in Karen Katz's lift-the-flap book.

Now, if you have ever made conversation/narrated a story to a baby, you will know that it is not the most natural thing in the world. Even if you have given birth to said baby. It is perfectly normal to feel silly while doing so. My jaws hurt from 'making funny faces' at the baby, which I did as I was told to do. But I didn't give up.

I'm Pregnant, Not Terminally Ill, You Idiot!

Baby Byte:
***If we don't respond to what you are doing,
STOP DOING IT!***

I still have recordings of my reading *The Disappearing Hats* or *The Gingerbread Man* from when Rehaan was a baby. Unless you are a voiceover artiste, MC or a radio jockey, you are not used to throwing your voice to such monstrous proportions all day. I just found it plain exhausting. Talking constantly in a high-pitched, baby sing-song way made my throat sore; and if that wasn't enough, the baby didn't particularly appreciate my performance either.

But I plodded on, my voice hoarse, hoping that one day, my antics will be rewarded, or at the very least, I could find an alternate career as baby-book-reader-and-performing-artist.

The only book he took to was Rod Campbell's *Dear Zoo*, another lift-the-flap book in which a little boy receives various animals from the zoo as presents, and has to return them because they are too big, or too jumpy or too tall. And a little squeaky book called *Eliot the Elephant*, in which Eliot loses his voice, and squeaks every time you touched him. It must be empowering for a little boy to make a grown elephant squeak!

Forget reading, I am going to talk to him, I thought. We will have a conversation, who needs books? Every time I attempted, he would wander off to do his own thing. When I sang, he thought I was psycho. When I told a story, he was more interested in my breasts. Purvi, who was a year ahead of me in babydom, had her two-bits to offer. 'I drew black squiggles on a white sheet of paper and showed it to Ayaan when he was six months. It really stimulates their visual sense.' I did as instructed. He ate the paper.

So one day, I gave up and decided, I am going to pretend the baby is a friend, we'll both do our thing, and give each other space. This worked out beautifully. Except that he defined my breasts as his space and came around to help himself whenever he wished. That was slightly unsettling. But otherwise, the strategy worked.

One day, while driving to town with the baby, I was stuck at this really mad jam, and was on second gear for the longest time. Just to amuse myself, I started reading hoardings on bus shelters aloud. I heard some clapping and cooing from behind. It was him! My baby! Being entertained by my voice! That is when it struck me. It was not about the books or the stories; he just wanted to hear my voice. As real and funny as it could get. Obviously I was faking it with the books, and the baby could tell.

Month fourteen and he was still not into books. But by this time, I was so into his books, that I couldn't care less. Someone then told me about the wondrous Eric Carle, and soon I had *A Very Grouchy Lady Bug*, *A Very Hungry Caterpillar* and *Brown Bears* of various sizes going to bed with me. He on the other hand, was taking saucepans, pressure cookers and ladles to bed.

A redeeming thing I figured in my baby-book journey was that the boy, quite like me, always wanted to read the last page first.

I realised that it hardly made a difference what kind of stimulus works for your baby. There are some who love books, some who want to eat them, and some who treat them as props. But they generally grow up to be literate. And they have their whole life to walk, talk, eat, count and recite stuff from books. Have you ever heard of a six-year-old who is not potty trained? Or who doesn't know the alphabet? So, if you were to stimulate your baby the way they teach you in baby books, you will be climbing walls, whether or not the baby does. In the end, it hardly makes a difference if your baby is eating solids in month five or eight, whether he is crawling in month six or nine, if he is walking in month ten or twelve, if he is talking in month twelve or fourteen. Babies do what they have to do when they want to do them.

16

Myth of the Hands-on Daddy

If marriage was skewed mathematics, having a baby takes it to another level. Every baby, by default, is born with a mother and a father, even if the only contribution made by the latter is a motile sperm who survived.

Fatherhood is a big deal for men. It's an affirmation of their manhood, relief that they are not firing blanks, joy at having produced something that somewhat looks like them (at least their own mothers think so) and pride at joining the approachable, yet exclusive fathers' club, a club they can inhabit for life.

Having successfully completed the mission of fathering, the next in line is the dirty work of fatherhood. This is where it gets tricky, and often, sticky, and the men are busy looking for their exit routes. After the first week of cooing over the baby, and aborted attempts at swaddling the baby, folding a cloth diaper, understanding the precise sound effects a burp constitutes, the men are off to do what they know best. Conquer the world. Mostly. Leaving all of the baby care to you.

Now whether you do it yourself or delegate it, it is still largely your problem. I didn't design this, and I was caught off-guard too, but it is. Of course men can be hands-on, as long as the hands are someone else's. When handed a baby, the only thought that's racing through their minds is, 'Who next can I hand it over to without making it look like I am lazy or inexperienced?'

It's not whether a man can change a diaper or give the baby a bath. It's how many diapers can he change and how many baths can he give before he manufactures a reason not to do it. When I asked my mommy friends about hands-on daddies, the reactions were mixed. Some stared blankly. Some laughed like their lungs would explode. Some chuckled in embarrassment. Some seethed in anger. Some looked like they would just burst a capillary. Some just shrugged. Some pretended not to know what I was talking about. And the rare one beamed with pride.

There seems to be some confusion about hands-on daddies. Changing a diaper doth not a hands-on daddy make. Doing it without being told comes close. What's a test is when the daddy is left alone with no help, no instructions and a child for say, one hour. And the child is awake.

Baby Byte:
Mommy, please give daddy a map of where everything is. It's not exactly cool lying on your back, letting it all hang when daddy goes on his diaper expedition.

Being hands-on also means knowing how to pack a baby bag. Essentially, it means knowing what the baby bag looks like and where the things that go into the baby bag are kept. It also means having the baby doctor's number on speed-dial and being able to tell when the baby is unwell. It means knowing when to change the baby's diaper, and doing it even without any instructions. It also means having at least three back-up ideas to distract the baby when it is in a bad mood. And above all, it means not asking, 'Does it need to be fed?' every time a crying baby is handed over. Or switching on the telly.

At a later stage, it means knowing who the baby's friends are and preferably having their numbers. Okay, the numbers of their parents. It means being able to rustle up something for the baby to eat if mommy is not home and the cook has bunked. It means not handing him a packet of chips. Or ordering from McDonald's. The point in men's favour is that they have an innate desire to protect, to provide for the family, to conquer. I realised that had I continued working full-time, I would have to negotiate support on a daily basis with the husband. So I made a deal with the husband that I provide the lion's share of care-giving while he provides the lion's share of the family income. The flip side is, he thought he was completely absolved of baby duty.

My friend Vishakha thought she was blessed. 'My husband does a lot compared to most other men I know. I am really lucky.'

'So what all does he do?' I asked, with a twinge of scepticism in my voice.

'Well, he changes diapers whenever he is around. He also offers to babysit whenever I have a meeting or event to go to.'

I informed her that you can't babysit your own baby, but she waved it off as a technicality. 'Also, whenever he is home early, he takes the baby for a walk in the pram,' she added.

'That's great! All by himself?' I couldn't help being the bitch.

'No, with the maid of course. You need help, come on!'

None of these tasks was routine. Help was available on an as-and-when-required basis. Her husband would do whatever he was asked to do whenever he was asked to do it, after he was told how to do it and for how long.

I was amused at her gratitude.

My problem was, I hated giving instructions. Making a list of things-to-do-for-daddy just felt wrong. I expected the husband to be a partner in parenting. To pick up the ball and run. To take the initiative. The most initiative he ever displayed was to buy us a baby monitor on day one of bringing the baby home. And the height of his contribution through the first eighteen months was offering to switch the monitor on every night or offering to play the baby's sleep music on the iPod.

I'm Pregnant, Not Terminally Ill, You Idiot!

My scepticism still intact, I asked another friend, Chaitali, about hands-on daddies She was quite matter of fact. 'You are asking the wrong person. I have zero experience with hands-on daddies. I don't know who they are.' She had two daughters, age four and eight, and a husband who put the pizza on the table, but was largely unavailable for hands-on parenting. Turns out her best friend's husband in America was the only hands-on daddy she knew.

A couple I know who works in computer consultancy staggered their shifts so that one of them could always be there for the baby. That was the most real example of a hands-on daddy I came across.

Another friend, Shefali, had a stay-at-home husband, who worked from home. The perception, of course, was that he was a great hands-on dad. I envied her. Once when I asked her for advice on how to distribute baby work so that it's fair, she said: 'Everything to do with child-care is your job! Do not expect anything from the man.'

'But I've heard your husband is really hands-on.'

'Yes, he is around most of the time. But I still do the work.'

My friend Deepa turned out to be really lucky on this score. When she went back to work, her husband had just quit his job and was starting on his own from home. She was at ease since the child was being monitored by her husband with the help of a baby-maid. 'He was also my main accomplice in the pumping business. There were times when I'd be so damn frustrated but if it weren't for him to keep me at it, my son would not have got his elixir. My mother was of no help in these matters since they never pumped in their time.'

'So what all does he do?' I had to find a loophole.

'He has managed to put him to sleep on more than one occasion, in his unique way of rocking and chanting! There are times when I am at my wit's end and couldn't be bothered about entertaining my son. At these times, he is fantastic in keeping him interestingly occupied.'

'What about food?' I asked.

'Yes, he also whips up some good stuff for him to eat.'

This can't be true. I am despondent. She can sense it.

'I think he has a shade more of the Ying than the Yang or maybe it has to do with him being a Gemini. But before we rush to crown him, let me also add that all of this can be done for short spells of time. Ask him to do this for a longer period and then of course, it's another story.'

Phew!

Vishakha who was grateful for her occasionally baby-sitting and pram-wheeling husband added, 'I think we are unduly hard on the men and perhaps we should just trust them more with baby-tasks rather than saying, "Oh, you will not be able to manage that."'

If he would only get up from that couch, or let go of that controller, I have all intentions of being benevolent, I thought to myself.

It's perfectly normal for new mothers to be angry at the fact that their lives have turned completely topsy-turvy while not much has changed for the man, except for the fact that he is a dad on paper. I used to think it legitimate that if the man made fifty percent contribution to the production of the baby, he should make at least a ten percent contribution in rearing it. Unfortunately, the math doesn't work that way for most women. Whenever I heard a mommy say, 'My husband is so involved, I wouldn't know what to do without him,' I would feel overcome by the desire to spy on them to figure out the catch in the situation (there had to be one).

All men start out fine. They have all these lofty ideals of being hands-on, often reminiscing that their fathers were not. But what most men don't get is that baby-care is something of an assembly line thing – there is a set of tasks that need to be done over and

over again, in pretty much the same way, to produce the same results. So making funny faces at the boy for three minutes a day and then saying, 'I really played with him today' doesn't count.

Throughout the pregnancy, my husband told me, 'Just wait till I become a daddy. I am going to change diapers, sing to the baby, tell it stories, rock it to sleep, burp, change and bathe the baby. Oh, I am going to love it all!'

I am sure he meant every word. He just didn't know that consistency was a prerequisite.

My friend Sheena's husband would walk into the house announcing, 'Please don't make me change diapers or burp the baby tonight. I've had a hard day.'

'And what about me? Do I look like I just stepped out of a manicure and blow-dry?' She would blurt. Sometimes.

But most of the times, she would just let it go, thinking, 'Oh, no, these are bad vibes for the baby. Be nice, be sweet.' This is the same man who was all gung-ho about being hands-on just a few months ago.

Men like picking up babies, because babies make them look good. But their threshold is four minutes. 'Is it time for a feed?' They will ask, even as they have barely picked up the baby. It will be their exit route for at least as long as the baby hasn't weaned. No wonder fathers always look harrowed when they are left with the baby for longer than five minutes. The biceps and triceps that sweep women off their feet are usually no good when it comes to picking up and lugging a cherub.

But what men are really good at is Instagram parenting. Put a smartphone or a few single women in the room and watch the men preen over their babies. They are happy to change the diaper, wear the baby, rock the baby, walk the baby, flip an omelette, do whatever it takes to make an impression. And of course they make good pictures for Facebook or those air-brushed parenting magazines that will lap up a dad rocking his baby to sleep. Even if only the mother knows it was for three of the 365 days.

But ask a man to put a fidgety baby to sleep on a regular day when no one is watching and start your stopwatch. The best of them will give up in seven minutes. The average bloke will last two.

Baby Byte:
The difference between mom and dad is that mom does the work even when no one is looking.

It's not about multi-tasking. It's about dealing with something that they don't know what to expect of. And we all know about men and the fear of the unknown. So I guess asking a guy who can't cook to make a soufflé would produce the same results as handing him a baby without a manual.

Yes, there are fears. 'What if I drop the baby?' is the first preoccupying thought in the man's head, at least when the child is an infant.

Let me help here. It is your baby. It is not a Ming vase or a crystal heirloom that you should be afraid of dropping. And the more you hold it, the better you will get at it. So try and not use the first opportunity to hand over the baby to someone else. That's the only way you will gain baby-holding confidence. So if you are pregnant, your husband better start working out now!

The *what ifs* continue and the men don't make it any easier by being all nervous and hyper and obsessive about every little thing. 'Oh, the baby is touching paper. Oh, the baby is putting paper in mouth. Oh, the baby is about to sneeze. Oh, the baby has sneezed. Oh the doorbell might ring and wake the baby up. Oh, the curtain may billow and the sun might come in and blind the baby. Oh, the fan is making too much noise, maybe it will wake him up?'

As the child grows older, the *what ifs* get more gory.

'What if the child pokes himself in the eye with the fork?'

'What if the mug drops and the child walks all over the shards and cuts himself and then walks all over the house bleeding?'

'What if the child eats the paper and the newsprint has something toxic that causes food poisoning and we have to rush to the hospital?'

'What if the child learns to unlock the bathroom door, turns on the taps, fills a bucket and drowns?'

'What if the child opens the front door and crawls out the door, onto the landing and eventually, leaves the building without our knowledge?'

I am not whining. The husband is loving, caring, means well, is deeply sensitive and appreciative of my efforts and has all intentions to make an effort. But he is just not qualified for some jobs, and managing a baby is one of them. Whenever he was given charge of putting the baby to sleep and it took him longer than five minutes, he would moan, 'It's easier for you, you have tits.'

'Oh really? You think having a baby suck on your tits for an average of an hour each time, several times a day is easy? You gotta be kidding!'

So there. One small task, and he has got you all wired up!

The funny thing is, you are a first-time parent too, and you are still figuring things out, but the men expect you to have all the answers. 'Why is he frantic? Why is he refusing to sleep? Why is he waking up so often?'

Yes, men can change diapers. It's just that it takes them seven minutes instead of one. Yes, they can change the baby's clothes. It's just that they don't know where they are kept, and each time you tell them, they still have trouble remembering. Yes, they can sing to the baby. Whenever in a mood, or really zoned out. Yes, they can prepare baby food. After being given instructions in triplicate, a map for where everything is, and with a few hours on hand. Yes, they can give the baby a bath. It's just that by the time they prepare the bath, which would involve checking the temperature of the water with a thermometer or some fancier device (provided they find it in the first place), loading the bath with toys and bath books that they think the baby might need, checking the temperature again and realising it has dropped (naturally), adding more hot water to balance it out, then realising the water is too much, and so draining some. And after all this, going in search of the baby, and realising it is not where they left it.

Please note that the baby's towel and change of clothes still haven't been put out. Nor have they any idea how to soap the baby or wash its face, forget the hair. Nor do they know that the threshold of the baby's patience while it is in the supine position (as it will be when it's put down to air or change) is exactly twenty seconds, so 'time is of essence'.

The tough part is when you leave the baby with the husband, and step out for an errand, like getting rid of the fuzz on your upper lip. You have to give c-l-e-a-r step-by-step instructions for what he is supposed to do and how he should do it. Also, a plan B, C and D. Nothing is a given. For instance, you could be going to a movie with your girlfriend and the film is two hours. Traffic, travel, parking time factored in, it's three hours. So for three hours, you have to tell the husband what he is supposed to be doing. Like for example: 'The baby is sleeping now. When he wakes up, check his diaper and change it if it's wet or soiled.' You will also need to explain how wet is wet and what soiled means. Then you will have to ask him to clean the baby (and the 'how' is important, whether wipes, cotton, water, just water, or water and wipes), dry him (again show how) and then put on a fresh diaper.

Coming to food. Say, the baby has to be given a banana. Telling him how the banana should be given is important. You must say, 'Peel it, mash it and give it with a spoon, a small spoonful at a time.' If you don't do that, you might come back to see a baby holding a whole banana, trying to figure out if it should be played with, eaten or thrown.

'Play with the baby' should also be spelt out as P-l-a-y *with* the baby. If you don't do that, you may come back to each of them doing their own thing. And you never know what the baby's *own* thing may be. Perhaps it's opening the fridge and pulling out all its contents.

And then you return. To find that the diaper is over-soaked and has leaked into his pyjamas. The baby is oblivious through it all, but so is the dad (who by now has handed over a remote to the baby and is busy fiddling with the other).

I have stopped asking the husband to do any baby-related work, because it just causes a capillary to burst in my head. He still asks me where his knickers are or what his porridge looks like. Does that make him a bad father? No.

Sure, we have all heard of men who are totally in charge and can beautifully manage the baby when you are not around, feed, burp, change, put baby to sleep, give it a bath, tuck him to sleep. All this without whining once. We just haven't seen them.

A friend told me that fathers are pretty useless until the baby starts communicating (read that as telling daddy what it wants or wants him to do). That's two years at best. If you do have a hands-on man at your disposal, well, congratulations! You've got that one in a million. Do everything in your power to keep him, and if possible loan him to distressed friends from time to time.

17
Work Bitches

Okay, you have made the baby. Question is, what next? Do you have a plan? Are you going to be a stay-at-home-mama? Are you going back to work? Have you figured out who is going to look after your little cherub? Have you/your partner negotiated flexible working hours or even the possibility of it? Have you found a maid, a day-care, a committed grandparent who will take charge of your child while you are away?

Or are you hoping for divine intervention?

There are ways and ways of negotiating motherhood, and there is no right or wrong about any of them really. There are those like my mother who get on with it, leaving the baby with family and formula (those were the glorious joint family days). She was a school teacher, so her hours were good. She loved her job and retired from the same school thirty-four years later.

There are others who do day-care, nannies, grandparents, or a combination thereof, depending on what their sanity or salary can afford. There are those, who like me, decide that jobs can be got back, but baby time can't, and plunge into full-time baby care.

If you do the former, you are often looked at sceptically as someone who chose career over motherhood, money over emotional bonding, bottle over breast.

If you choose the latter, you are looked upon as someone who was using motherhood as an excuse to sit at home and 'do nothing', who is an emotional sucker waiting to be manipulated by her child, who wanted out of the rat race and has found her way. Not that quitting work is an option for most women – you need a partner who is willing to put the bread on the table, sometimes jam and cheese too, for an indefinite period of time, while you play primary caregiver to the baby.

So damned if you do and damned if you don't.

Your reasons for going back could be as compelling as your reasons for staying at home. Money, of course is the biggest reason, considering that two incomes are better than one, now that there is an additional member in the family. But the mathematics of being a stay-at-home mother are quite different for a woman who has a baby at say twenty-three, or one who has it at thirty-nine. For one, the monies at stake are much higher, the career graph is at a different place. There is much more to give up – lifestyle, a fancy home, exotic holidays, Ivy League schools for the child, designer wear for you.

While the twenty-three-year-old mommy will hardly be missed at her workplace; the same will not be true for the thirty-nine-year-old. Her role would be more pivotal, her meter ticking with greater intensity, and the company is busy computing the losses it incurs on account of her being away.

You could well be the one-in-a-million woman whose husband opts to (and can) be a stay-at-home daddy. Otherwise, men never have to deal with sticky negotiations and parenting issues on the work front. They are as good as new, post fatherhood and nothing really changes about their life, work or otherwise. Your working life, on the other hand will be a negotiation on a daily basis. The maid doesn't turn up. Who takes the day off? The baby is sick. Who stays home? The baby has to be picked up from day-care. Who rushes out from office? Nine out of ten times, it is you.

The Indian Labour Law prescribes a compulsory paid maternity leave of twelve weeks to all female employees. No company is liable to offer anything more. If they do, it is an act of philanthropy. Most companies treat motherhood as some sort of hobby or incurable disease the woman has suddenly developed and not as a natural progression of single to married to pregnant to mother. I have heard, of course, that a few corporates, IT companies, banks and NGOs are empathetic about this transition and do offer extended leave, sabbaticals, flexitime options, consultancy options and even day-care facilities. But it is still a small minority. By and large, women have come to terms with the fact that yes, there are compromises post baby and putting career on hold is probably one of them. One mommy who quit her high-ranking job soon after the baby, was magnanimous enough to say that she didn't expect the organisation to make those compromises for her, nor did she expect to be paid for having a child.

I was shocked at the lack of dissent.

I felt a ray of hope hearing Vineeta's story. Both the companies she worked for since her pregnancy and through her child's infancy (who is now four) had day-care, the option to work flexitime, and extended leave of up to six months. 'I was lucky,' she said. 'But why should it be about luck or being blessed? Why can't companies factor in motherhood when hiring women and have policies laid down so that it's not a case-to-case negotiation with one's superior? Why can't pregnancy and motherhood be treated as a natural phase of a working woman's life?' My friend Amrita who runs a day-care says she has seen a significant change in company policies in the eight years since she began her service. More and more had day-cares onsite, a few were considering flexitime options as a mode to keep women from quitting. It's a start, no doubt.

But elsewhere, companies still have an all-or-none policy and are largely unwilling to negotiate working terms for a new mother. I have known several women who were forced to quit as a result of this. 'It is not a part of the company policy,' they are told. 'We can't make an exception for you.' It is as though organisations do not want to acknowledge the logistics that comes with motherhood; it is treated as a sort of exotic inconvenience and they would rather you deal with it separately from work. It's tough to fathom how companies with a fifty percent female workforce have no contingency plan for new mothers. Like it was some natural calamity they were totally unprepared for.

So one fine day, the maternity leave reaches its expiry date and extensions are no longer possible. You have used up all your leave categories like sick leave, privilege leave and casual leave. Your mother has reached fatigue point and is threatening to leave and your third baby-maid in three months has just quit. And it's time to go to work.

One of the first things that strikes you when you go back to work is that the honeymoon is over – you are no longer pregnant and cute, this means you are no longer wearing your baby on your sleeve, so you no longer enjoy the small privileges that came with it – like excusing yourself from an utterly pointless video conference because you were feeling sick, or had a sonography appointment.

No matter how resilient you are, most women are in shock at the callousness at work on returning from their maternity leave. In several subtle and not-so-subtle ways, being pregnant at the workplace seems to indicate that you no longer 'count', that you are now just someone who is 'passing through', that you may or may not continue working, that you might be 'too preoccupied with baby thoughts' to focus on your career. What you don't realise is that right from the time you were pregnant, the tone for your eventual marginalisation has been set. If it can happen to an Aishwarya Rai Bachchan, it can happen to you.

Soon, friends and family do their bit to ease you out of the trauma of the impending decision. 'Maybe you can work part-time? I know someone who works from home.'

Yes, but what they don't know or care to find out is that the math is distorted. For instance, the 'flexitime' option might require you to take a fifty percent pay cut. Negotiating for flexitime is like letting your guard down (*I am needy. Exploit me!*). Part-time might just mean fewer hours with the same workload and lesser pay. And settling for less money, almost no power, and the same amount of work is not a great feeling. At least when your heart is still where the baby cot is.

Sonia, who wasn't as 'lucky' as Vineeta, returned to her banking job post baby on a half-day deal for the first month post maternity leave. She soon sensed a resentment from her single female colleagues and those who didn't have kids. There was no reason for the resentment, since the half-day also translated to half-pay, so it wasn't like she was enjoying special privileges. The work atmosphere grew increasingly unpleasant and the hostility with fellow female colleagues grew. 'Just because I had to leave at 6 p.m., I didn't think I had to prove to anyone that I was equally serious about my job as they were.' She soon changed jobs, but then realised that the more things changed, the more they stayed the same. She also did a stint with an NGO in the interim and found that the empathy was reassuring. 'They are kinder places for women who have just given birth. If you don't have help, you are always allowed to bring the child to work and it is not frowned upon.'

Three years since, Sonia still thinks that Indian companies have a long way to go in supporting new mothers to stay at their jobs.

To all those women who had independent minds, great careers, and fat pay checks pre-baby, welcome to the other side. The great middle.

I keep hearing of women who 'work from home'. 'This friend of mine works for two hours a day, uploads content for some fancy website and gets paid really well,' said someone. 'In your field, freelancing is really easy, no?' asked an aunt. I still have to find out what these websites and these well-paying freelance jobs are.

Just before I went on maternity leave, I had a glimpse into my future at work. A new mommy returned after her three-month maternity leave, hoping to get an extension. She was in for a rude shock when she was told that it wouldn't be possible, neither was flexitime an option. It was all or none. Since she was still in her postpartum melancholia, and hadn't yet figured out baby-care and other such, she did the first thing that came to her mind – she quit.

Two months later, the same thing happened to another mommy.

'We don't want to set a precedent,' both were told, although the nature of their jobs could have easily allowed flexitime. That is the funniest thing I have heard. It conjured up images of all the women in the organisation thronging to claim maternity perks.

Unless you are self-employed or have Big Daddy looking out for you at your place of work, or you work for the UNICEF or the four-and-a-half companies with souls I mentioned earlier, most new mothers have a not-so-pleasant place to go back to – no matter how big the organisation or how long you have been there. The fact is most companies don't know how to deal with the 'strange' needs of new mothers. Of having to nurse. Or expressing milk. Or bringing their baby to work. Or being excused for an hour in the afternoon so they can go home or to the day-care and check on their babies. There's all this talk about *really not wanting to lose you*, but then, they aren't exactly doing anything to make it easy for you either. I guess I too was 'lucky' that my HR department granted me access to a private room for expressing milk, post my return from maternity leave. At least that solved part of my problem...a big part, now that I look back or read emails on my mommy network from women who have no facility to express at work and hence have to force-wean their babies.

When the bump is gone, you are no longer to be fussed over, in fact the sooner you get in line with the rest, the better it is for you. It is ironic that although a new mother is physically much weaker than the pregnant mother, concessions are made for the latter, but not for the former. After the initial, 'Oh, how cute is your baby,' it's down to brass tacks. 'Now enough of the work concessions, bitch! We have suffered enough with your protruding belly. Don't give us your baby stories now, please!'

My mind was made up. I would quit, but only after giving it one real shot of balancing work and baby. I needed to do that for myself. I needed to be sure. Since my mother had committed to spending six months with me, I still had time. I wanted to do it without feeling cornered into it.

Incidentally, when I returned from maternity leave, I was at first shocked, and then relieved to find out that I had been transferred from a pivotal role with one section of the paper to a not-so-pivotal one in another section, a fact told to me rather casually on the phone a few days before resuming work. My new boss was clearly not happy to see me; evidently she had no say in the matter of my transfer. 'So why did you opt for this section?' she asked.

'I didn't,' I said. 'I wasn't asked, I was told.'

It was not a great way to begin.

She asked me nothing about the baby, how I was doing, or coping. Instead, she said, 'I actually thought you wouldn't come back. I stayed home for eight years after my daughter was born. Do you really need the job?'

It was not the greatest welcome back line, but I swallowed it.

The new role was a blessing in disguise though. I figured the job was less gruelling, did not involve daily production duties on the newspaper, because it was a weekend supplement, I didn't have to report at 9.30 a.m., so I thought it would be less taxing on the baby. I didn't make a noise about the transfer.

But I remember being made to wait till 12.30 a.m. on production nights even when I was not 'critical' to the scene and could have been easily spared the agony of being separated from my newborn for so long.

'If I let you go, everyone else will start expecting such privileges,' she said. Who everyone, I wondered? As far as I could see, there was not a single active womb around me. Who, then, was she talking about?

So much for thinking that female bosses would be more empathetic towards new mothers.

I worked for the next two months, expressing at work to keep up my baby's milk supply, feeling guilty about leaving baby-care entirely to my mother, especially on late nights, and feeling slightly resentful that my husband's life had remained unchanged. Yes, the money was good, and I did enjoy working, but when I extrapolated my life for the next two years, I found myself getting pulled in all directions. Besides, what after mom went back? I didn't want to do a day-care in haste. I hadn't done enough research. There was no plan B in sight.

So with a calm and collected mind I decided. This is it.

The reactions were mixed. The mommies who balanced work and baby (not so harmoniously) looked dismissive and warned me I would be bored in six months. The single men looked at me like I was off to be a suicide bomber. The daddies nodded in approval. The single women, surprisingly, wanted to be in my shoes. One told me, 'I wish I was in your place. Man. Marriage. Baby. You are sorted.' I was foxed. She was in her early twenties and I thought her generation of women was burning with ambition.

My family applauded me. My mother thought I was a martyr. My aunts couldn't stop gushing over how I had quit such a great job to be a mother. It was something they all wanted to do in their time, but couldn't. Some friends lauded me, others envied me.

A friend of mine pointed out that by spending time rearing her child, a mother is actually contributing to the country's GDP, because it is these children who will add to the productivity of the nation. But instead of being rewarded for her effort, the mother is penalised. Yes, there is always that murmur of 'working from home', but I have to yet see a respectable organisation putting it into practice or paying fairly for it. 'Flexitime' jobs in the market seem to be euphemisms for 'this job is so dull, you may want to throw up'.

One baby website that reviewed baby products, ironically called *mommyknowsall* or some such offered me an assignment. They said they would pay Rs 100 per review. They also stated that they regularly gave away freebies, usually baby stuff, making it look like a great perk of the job. I told them I wouldn't even fart for that amount. They were shocked. They didn't think mothers should do this for the money anyway.

Almost six months after I quit, I was approached by a deathly-dull industry magazine. The words that drew me were 'flexitime' and 'work from home'. As the discussion veered towards number of hours, I was told, 'Well, it's a full-time job in spirit. Almost 24x7. But yes, you can work from home once a week.'

'You are on call all the time,' is what I heard.

He asked me to name a figure. I asked him to name his (I was still reeling under the Rs 100 per review). He mentioned something that was less than half my previous salary. I told him to fly a kite. No, I didn't, but I wish I had. A few months later, I ran into him at a magazine launch. He looked the other way.

A few months later, a foreign travel magazine launching in India approached me for an issue editor's position. Their offer was seventy percent of my last salary. The commute was seventy percent more. I declined. They were confused. They couldn't fathom how someone in a position such as mine could say no to such a great offer.

Of course, being a full-time mom is tougher than it sounds.

For one, you are doing baby-duty 24x7 without a salary, and it is largely thankless. My friend warned me of the dangers. 'Men never really know how to measure the productivity of a woman when she is doing intangible things like managing a house or a baby.' So I asked my husband to pay me a salary, just to make me feel good.

Yes, there will also be friends who will ask you, 'So, what do you do all day?' Some will take you for granted and assume you are either getting your nails done or taking afternoon naps. Like Fauzia, who was always asking me to 'pick up movie tickets'. When she did it more than thrice, I said to myself, *Wait a minute, she has a car and a driver. Does she really think I am sitting around doing nothing, just because I have quit my job?*

Perhaps she did.

Baby Byte:
Don't ask my mommy what she does all day. Ask me.

But one good thing that comes out of all this is forced entrepreneurship. Some women make cookies and cupcakes. Others start puppetry workshops. Some float CSR initiatives and HR consultancies. I decided to write books. It was always a dream. The baby made it legitimate.

The jobs didn't dry up, even though I was hardly out in the market. But when it got into the numbers stage, companies wanted their pound of flesh in exchange for offering me, a new mother, the opportunity. A leading fashion magazine's financial controller once offered me a lower designation and pay-packet. 'But your resume shows a break, so it's only fair,' he said.

'I wasn't "taking a break". I was giving birth,' I told him.

So much for GDP, I thought. Companies were using motherhood

as a tool to get 'cheaper talent'. Perhaps mothers would bite it; they think it's going to be slim pickings anyway.

I made up my mind. I was not going back to work if it was not on my terms. I would write this book. For the next two years, when someone asked me what I did, I said I was on a baby and book project. It felt good.

I still got asked about when I planned to go back to work. My answer was, when I find a company that treats motherhood as 'normal' and not something you do on the sly.

18
When Does It Get Better?

It's almost futile to start a countdown on when you can have your life back once the baby is born. Technically, you never can. At least not the same life you left behind. The men of course get back to their lives in a few days after they are done responding to the congratulatory messages, uploading photos on the web of the newborn in their arms. Or when the dismal paternity leave (of a generous two weeks, tops) comes to an end. After the first few weeks of cosmetic parenting and holding the baby ever-so-gently, the dads get on with their lives. I hear there are fathers who take time-offs/sabbaticals post baby, but I am still to meet them.

It just takes infinitely long for mothers. Five years. Maybe ten. Or more. And even then, it doesn't end. It never does – whether you choose to stay at home or go back to work.

There are theories and theories about parenting. You will never know what works until something doesn't work.

If you have a partner who is equally hands-on, consider yourself lucky. But for a significant number of women who have to mostly fend for themselves, it is pretty damn hard, job or no job.

But in the whole managing your baby and your life, there are two things:

Do you want to get the baby out of the way, get your body back, life back, go to work, socialise, travel, and pretend that life goes on?

Do you want to get real?

The truth is, the baby is here to stay. And it will only get bigger and louder and soon will have a mind of its own. Today he is teething or refusing to be tucked into bed at 9 p.m. Tomorrow it will be, 'Why do I have to turn five to have the X Box Kinect?'

There is no way out, so you might as well see the humour in the situation.

Every phase of the baby is a new challenge, and the challenges only multiply, never subtract. There's infancy, when the needs are mostly physical. There's toddlerhood when the needs are cerebral and emotional. There's the socially challenging school-going phase. The teens, when the needs are cerebral and psychological. Then that phase when you don't even know why you are needed, but you need to be around. There is never a time when you can stop being a mother. One milestone attained, and there are hundreds to go.

I guess it's easier if you have your mother or mother-in-law living with you, but considering that we are generally having babies later in life, our mothers are much older and therefore, not totally fit to be hands-on (and looking after a baby requires immense physical strength). They, on the other hand, had the bounty of the joint family (however evil it seemed to be at that point) working for them and could go back to work with a clearer conscience.

I had a friend I often marvelled at. She had twins, aged ten-and-a-half, and both she and her husband had full-time demanding jobs; she as a magazine editor and he as a research scientist. She told me that the longer I delayed getting back to work, the harder it would get. Or so I thought. On the face of it, she was cool, business-like, brisk, efficient, always on top of things. 'The way to do it was to get your support systems in place, have three maids instead of one, reward them well, be hands-off and not get in their way much. Also, make sure at least one parent is always on call in case of an emergency.' She had it all figured out.

But once, while I was having lunch with her, one of her twins called. She looked at me sheepishly and said, 'I have to take this. It is the fifth time he is calling.' She proceeded to have a melt-down on the phone about not being there to help him with his science project. 'I am so sorry, baby. I will come home and help you tonight. Promise.' She was pleading.

So things are not always what they seem to be, I thought. Evidently, she was paying a price for staying in the race, and it seemed unfair. Strangely, fathers don't go through the same struggle. Fatherhood is largely invisible, unless a man wears it on his sleeve or on his soft board at work. Unless paternity leave changes into something more respectable than one week, fathers will never feel that they are an equal party in the whole parenting thing.

Everyone has their own theory of when it (motherhood) gets easier. The theories range from extreme feminism (*Don't get ensnared by the whole motherhood thing, go on, get your life back!*) to extreme patriarchy (*Only a mother can truly bring up a child*). Each theory exists because it suited someone who articulated it.

Mine is to have a baby only when you are in a position to take a few years off from your career, because it is the only way you can be sure you did everything you could or wanted to, especially if both you and your partner are in high-pressure jobs with no fixed exit hours, commute long distances and don't live with family. I may be raising a few feminist hackles here, but this is what I think. It's true that children grow up anyway and they turn out pretty okay in the end. I guess I did too, but my mother still wishes she had been 'there' for me more than she did.

Everyone has a theory of when baby-care gets better:

'The first three months are the best. The baby is either feeding or sleeping.'

'The first three months are the worst. You are just a milk machine. After that, it only gets better.'

'Once the baby starts communicating, it gets better.'

'Enjoy as much as you can now. Once he starts walking about, you've had it.'

'The first two years are the most important. If you can take time off, that's when you should.'

'It hardly matters if you are around in the first two years. Almost anyone will do. It is when they start talking and communicating that they really need you, and at that time, the nanny or your mother might not be enough stimulation.'

But I think the most honest words came from my friend Vasu. 'No matter how much your kids grow up, you never really stop being a mother.'

Perhaps she is right. Being a mother is an irreversible process. Of course your working friends will goad you into getting your life back. 'Once he starts playschool, you can get back to work', or 'If you don't get back to work in six months, you never will.' To each, her own.

I have complete respect for mothers who manage career, baby, home and social life, but I didn't see myself as one of them. I opted out of the race for superwoman. I couldn't see myself as someone who is always a clock watcher, who palpitates every time she gets a call from home, who calls in every half hour to check on how her baby is doing, whose only preoccupying thought on stepping in to work is when can she step out, who is wondering whether the maid is eating the baby's apples, who is constantly negotiating with the husband to get him to 'do more'. I was willing to stay in oblivion till things settled down into a rhythm of their own (I am not sure when that happens).

I would rather be in one place than two, so I quit and decided to write full-time as my baby grew. I had also reached a point when the baby was more stimulating than any job. I guess I could afford to quit because my partner was gallant enough to be an indefinite provider for the family.

Since I had always been a good multi-tasker, I didn't think the baby would really get in the way of my productivity. I would write my weekly column, freelance a bit, work on that book, do my yoga. What can stop me, I asked myself?

I forgot one small detail. I was alone. (The baby-maid took me fourteen months to find.) The husband usually surfaced from work just before the baby went to sleep, and had a nervous breakdown every time he had to hold the baby for more than sixty seconds. There were sporadic maids, but I was largely left to fend for myself. Which is perhaps when mundane tasks began to seem mammoth.

So, I went to bed and I was alone (the husband was unwinding with the remote control in the other room). I woke up and I was alone (he was in slumber land). Occasionally, he did change diapers (when the time and place was convenient, or if he could find them), or walked the baby. Only to complain that his wrists hurt and would I please take over?

But there is no optimal time when you can let the baby be and get on with your life. At least no one has been able to do the math yet. There is the 'Babies may cry for a few days, but then they learn to adapt to anything' theory that is usually a way out for anyone wanting out and handing baby over to the next care-giver.

Preeta, my friend who saw life in power-point, told me I should quit after two years, because she believed that until then, it hardly matters who the caregiver is. 'All babies want is to be fed, burped, rocked, held periodically and it doesn't matter who does it. So if you can muster a maid, your mother, your mother-in-law, a nanny, a day-care, just do it, and get out and go to work. I was at home for six months and went nuts.'

'But what about the physical closeness which strengthens the emotional bond?' I wondered.

'Highly overrated,' she said.

I had to take her at face value. After all, she had a three-year-old, she was ahead in the game.

'But what about nursing?' I asked plaintively.

'Express!'

Now this is a word that is not to be used casually and it can only be done by someone who has not spent too much time expressing. It is big enough to have an entire chapter on it (Read *Much Ado About the Boob*), so you can imagine.

Parul, my unsolicited guide through pregnancy and thereafter said, 'The fun begins when they start talking. Till then, it's mostly work. But once they turn two, they are fun.'

Turns out, my fun days are here.

Shraddha from my yoga class said, 'What you do or don't do in the first two years for your child decides it all. By the time the child is two, the damage is done. Nothing that you do after that really counts. So if you have to choose a time when you want to give your life and career second priority, it is the first two years of your child.'

Clearly, I was being pulled in all directions.

Babies of course have their own agenda. Some, like mine, decide to be total delights in the first three months, sleeping through the nights, clocking in seven to eight hours, not being bothered by colic, burping when required, nursing well, making you feel that you have indeed made a dream baby and spoiling you silly.

And one fine day, it all changes. At first it is waking up every two hours in the night. Then it is every hour. And sometimes, it is asking you to nurse, sing, rock, play music, all at once before they decide to fall asleep again. When the teething demons arrive, they are at it for at least eighteen months.

Baby Byte:
Never tell anyone you have us all figured out. You will never get there.

Technically, when they say it gets easier after they go to school, I guess they are referring to the time that babies become children in the official sense, that is conform to the norms of societal behaviour and manners.

Men of course have no clue how the whole baby-growing-up thing happens seamlessly, as if on auto-pilot, and often, at work and social circles are known to exchange the following:

Guy 1: *So how old is the baby?*
Guy 2: *Four months.*
Guy 1: *So has your wife gone back to work yet?*
Guy 2: *Not for a few months, the baby is not ready yet.*
Guy 1: *Strange. My wife went back to work in three months.*
Guy 2: *Really?*

Men wouldn't know. They don't do the work, remember? And even if they did, the actual physical time a man spends with baby is nowhere close to what the woman does. It's not their fault, nature just designed it this way. And the non-existent paternity leave perhaps validates it. Which is why a male boss, even if he has children, doesn't quite get it when a subordinate can't really get herself together post maternity leave. There may be exceptions, but most of them don't.

When couples are biting their nails in anticipation of the baby, going on their last holiday as a 'twosome', setting up their nursery and thinking baby names, they are told, 'It's just the first three months, and then it's a breeze.'

When couples grapple with moody toddlers, they are told, 'Didn't I tell you the first year is the best?'

And when mothers withdraw into a shell post baby and diapers, it is not because they have nothing to say. It is not even because all they can talk about is potty and diapers. It is because at some level, they are angry no one ever told them their lives would turn so upside down in a not-so-nice-I-can't-find-myself way. It is also because someone somewhere finds this funny. And that person might even be a parent for all you know.

I still cannot say which has been the hardest part, but I have had moments every day when I felt exhilarated and moments when I felt real low. But in retrospect, I feel that when your body regains its strength, which can take six weeks to six months, your mind tends to function better. Things don't seem that intimidating and uphill and so, your ability to be positive, strong and resilient improves tremendously. That doesn't mean that things get easier.

Months can go by and one day when you are at a movie with your girlfriends, you receive a panic call from your husband. 'Can you come home right now? He has been wailing for ten minutes non-stop and I'm losing my mind. I just don't know what to do. I think he needs you.'

Or you could be at work and the maid could call you to say that your ten-month-old has just eaten a bar of soap. Or he could be eight years old and has locked himself in the bathroom. Any which way, *you* are always on call. For a long, long time. Husbands have meetings, remember?

Epilogue

No one told me this

I know what you are thinking. *Why doesn't anyone ever talk about this stuff?*

All you ever hear is the ominous *Don't worry. It gets better* whenever you are having a meltdown as a new mother.

Or a sadistic, *Make the most of it now. Very soon, it will only be susu-potty!* when you announce you are pregnant.

Before you give birth, you have the notion of this perfect birth, where you are in the hands of angels, feel joy instead of pain, and come out of it like a breeze, holding a baby in your arms, that has the gentlest smile and even gentler demeanour. But for ninety-nine percent of the women, the bubble bursts somewhere along and a great majority are caught in a 'What just happened to me?' feeling.

Recently, a strange thing happened. I had two mothers and their babies over for a play-date at my apartment. One had an eighteen-month-old and the other had a two-and-a-half-year-old. On the surface, the children were happy, the mothers were at ease, and it was all about the 'here' and 'now'.

And then something led to something and within a few hours, each of the mothers was spilling out horror stories – of their birth, of the interventions, about how futile and helpless and powerless they felt, about issues with latching on that they faced, about postnatal woes, about episiotomies gone awry, about how there was no help at hand, about how hard they had to fight to breastfeed their own baby, and how, if they were to do it all over again, they resolved to be more empowered, ask the questions, find the answers beforehand so that they wouldn't be caught off-guard.

The funny thing is, I had met one of the two mothers at a

I'm Pregnant, Not Terminally Ill, You Idiot!

yoga class when I had just emerged from my postpartum exile, and still recovering from the aftermath of my C-section. In casual conversation, I asked her how her birthing experience was. She said, rather nonchalantly, 'Giving birth is easier than having a tooth extracted.' I hated her for that.

Why didn't she tell me she almost bled to death post her episiotomy then? Why didn't she tell me her son took ten weeks to latch on, and while she waited, she was dying of pain with her engorged breasts and her sore bottom? What was the need to sound so ethereal and blissed-out then? And why was she telling me the gory details now, eighteen months later, I wondered.

Well there are reasons and there are theories, and it's all a bit complicated and layered. But here is mine. As women, we have historically been conditioned not to voice our pregnancy or post-birth angst. To be in denial about our pain and to carry its burden, quietly, uncomplainingly, stoically. It's what mothers do, we are told.

Women have been taught to 'numb the pain' through centuries. It's something everyone goes through, something that is not meant to be expressed, something to be internalised, something to be fought and won over, but never talked about. It is as though pain is our lot.

And so mothers are in mourning for the longest time. Until someone picks on a scab, and it all comes gushing out. Like it did with this fellow mom I knew.

Every woman thinks she will be the odd one out if she appears anything less than ethereal after having given birth. More so if she whines or expresses anger at the state of things, at being short-changed, at feeling disempowered during childbirth.

She is so wrong. Even Julia Roberts and Angelina Jolie came out of the hospital looking and feeling like wrecks. Just that no paparazzi shot them, for fear of being sued by the celebrities.

And yet, every woman wants to believe that she is one-up in

the motherhood curve, that she has won, conquered her demons, achieved her milestones, overcome her hurdles, and has, most importantly, turned from woman to mother.

It's like this. Pregnancy and motherhood is a ride that starts the minute you discover you are pregnant and continues until after the baby is born. From giving birth to becoming a mother is a long journey and a very slow one. Although we are meant to be naturals, it is so not true. Giving birth doth not a mother make.

There is always a cross to bear. If you've had no problem conceiving, you could have problems in the first trimester – morning sickness, high acidity, general lethargy, food allergies. Or worse, a miscarriage.

If so far so good, then the second or the third trimester might be complicated.

Or you might have to have an amniocentesis.

Or you might put on too much weight. Or too little.

And then you wait for your due date. And then the baby may not engage. Or you may not go into labour. Or your contractions may not be far apart. Or your dilation may not be enough. And the doctor starts ringing the C-sec alarm bells or threatens to induce labour.

If the birth is okay, then the baby might have trouble latching on.

If that's okay, your stitches might hurt like crazy.

Or you might be making too little milk. Or too much.

But motherhood is an exile. The more time you spend with yourself and the baby, the clearer things become, the better you become capable of dealing with them. Like you needed this catharsis, and only you can help yourself.

And yet...

There is nothing that comes close to the joy of holding a baby in your hands. A baby that you made and nurtured for nine months.

There is nothing more visually delightful than the transition from black to greenish black to yellow brown to canary yellow potty on a nappy, indicating that all is well.

There is no bigger thrill than watching baby milestones – the first time the baby turns, the first time he crawls, the first time he holds on to things, his first tooth, his first smile, his first solid food, the first time he walked, the first words he uttered.

There is nothing more warm and fuzzy than the gurgling sounds of a baby when he is breastfeeding.

There is no greater satisfaction than having given a baby a good burp.

And finally, there is nothing like knowing that you have finally found the purest form of love ever known.

Acknowledgements

I always thought this would be the easiest bit to write, but it's not. If I have forgotten some names, please blame it on motherhood malaise and know that you are thanked too.

So first, to Dee, my partner in creation; I owe you for keeping up with my hormones, good and bad, through pregnancy and after. For always believing the book will rock, even before it was written. For margaritas and massages.

Mita, my agent who flogged me till I got it right.

Vikram, in whose home-office most of this book was written and edited. I owe you for conversation, tea, food and wifi. And yes, cats.

To every single friend who told me they would buy the book and gift it too.

Prachi, Aparna, Iris, Deepa, Sameera, Yasmin, Aaraty, Rama, Amruta, for reading bits and pieces of the manuscript and giving it the nod.

Priya for giving it a hawkeye, and reminding me to be politically correct.

To every mommy who had a story to tell.

Rashmi, friend, editor and fellow-mommy who treated the book as she would a baby.

Bhavana and Aditya, for adding so much zest through their illustrations.

Jerry, friend and mentor who taught me most of what I know about writing and books.

And lastly my son Re—for all the gurgles, smiles, laughs and sighs that propelled me to write this book. You are even more fun outside the belly as you were inside it.